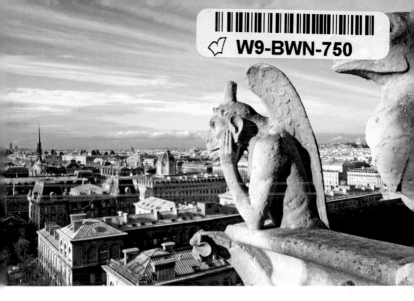

Introduction

Paris—the City of Light—has been a beacon of culture for centuries. As a world capital of art, fashion, food, literature, and ideas, it stands as a symbol of all the fine things human civilization can offer. Come prepared to celebrate this, rather than judge our cultural differences, and you'll capture the romance and joie de vivre that Paris exudes.

Paris offers sweeping boulevards, chatty crêpe stands, chic boutiques, and world-class art galleries. Sip decaf with deconstructionists at a sidewalk café, then step into an Impressionist painting in a tree-lined park. Climb Notre-Dame and rub shoulders with the gargoyles. Cruise the Seine, zip up the Eiffel Tower, and saunter down Avenue des Champs-Elysées. Master the Louvre and Orsay museums. Save some after-dark energy for one of the world's most romantic cities.

17e

BLVD. DE COURCELLES

Parc de Monceau

To La Défense &
La Grande Arche →

JACQUEMART-
ANDRE MUSEUM

GARE
ST. LAZARE

RUE ST. LAZARE

GALERIES
LAFAYETTE

BLVD. HAUSSMANN

BLVD. HAUSSMANN

9e

**ARC DE
TRIOMPHE**

AVE. KLEBER

AVE. DES CHAMPS-ELYSEES

RUE LA BOETIE

LA
MADELEINE

OPERA
GARNIER

16e

8e

Place
Vendôme

PALAIS
ROYAL

To
Marmottan
Museum →

GRAND
PALAIS

Place de
la Concorde

RUE DE RIVOLI

ARCHITECTURE &
MONUMENTS MUSEUM

PETIT
PALAIS

1e

TROCA-
DERO

CAFE
CARLU

RIVER
CRUISES

ORANGERIE

ORANGERIE

Tuileries
Garden

LOUVRE

RIVER
CRUISES

QUAI DES TUILERIES

Seine

MARITIME
MUSEUM

SEWER
TOUR

QUAI
D'ORSAY

Esplanade
des Invalides

ORSAY

**EIFFEL
TOWER**

RUE ST. DOMINIQUE

7e

ARMY MUSEUM
& NAPOLEON'S
TOMB

**L E F T
B A N K**

RUE DE SEINE

BLVD. ST. GERMAIN

**RUE
CLER**

AVE. DE LA
MOTTE-PICQUET

RODIN
MUSEUM

BLVD. RASPAIL

Parc du
Champ de
Mars

AVE. DE SUFFREN

AVE. DE TOURVILLE

ST. SULPICE

RUE DE RENNES

To RER Rail
&
VERSAILLES

AVE. DE VILLARS

Luxembourg
Garden

RUE D'ASSAS

15e

ECOLE
MILITAIRE

6e

BLVD. GARIBALDI

RUE DE SEVRES

RUE DE VAUGIRARD

GARE
MONTPARNASSE

**MONTPARNASSE
TOWER**

MONTPARNASSE
CEMETERY

→ To Catacombs

MAP LEGEND

Use this legend to help
you navigate the maps
in this book.

Ⓜ Metro Stop

Ⓡ RER Station

🅱 Batobus / Boat Stop

🅑 Bus Stop

🅟 Parking

Ⓣ Taxi Stand

⧫ View Point

■ Point of Interest

✦ Entrance

WC Restroom

Rick Steves'

POCKET

PARIS

Rick Steves, Steve Smith & Gene Openshaw

Contents

To Montmartre & Sacré-Cœur

GARE DU NORD

GARE DE L'EST

Canal St-Martin

RUE LAFAYETTE

BLVD. DE MAGENTA

BLVD. DE STRASBOURG

10e

BLVD. ST-DENIS

BLVD. ST-MARTIN

BLVD. DE BELLEVILLE

1/2 Kilometer
1/2 Mile

RIGHT BANK

2e

Place de la République

AVE. DE LA REPUBLIQUE

FORUM DES HALLES

RUE DU TEMPLE

3e

BLVD. BEAUMARCHAIS

PICASSO MUSEUM

BLVD. VOLTAIRE

PÈRE LACHAISE CEMETERY

POMPIDOU

JEWISH MUSEUM

Place du Châtelet

HOTEL DE VILLE

MARAIS

RIVER CRUISES

CARNAVALET MUSEUM

RUE ST-ANTOINE

Place des Vosges

SAINTE-CHAPELLE

Ile de la Cité

HOLOCAUST MEMORIAL

Place de la Bastille

BLVD. ST-MICHEL

NOTRE-DAME

Ile St. Louis

4e

OPERA

Place de la Nation

CLUNY MUSEUM

PONT DE SULLY

SORBONNE

5e

River

PROMENADE PLANTEE

LATIN QUARTER

RUE MONGE

BLVD. DIDEROT

AVE. DAUMESNIL

PANTHEON

RUE MOUFFETARD

GARE D'AUSTERLITZ

GARE DE LYON

	Tourist Info		Stairs
	Church		Walk/Tour Route
1e	Arrondissements (Districts)		Trail
	Park		Railway
	Pedestrian Zone		Fountain

Introduction

About This Book

With this book, I've selected only the best of Paris—admittedly, a tough call. The core of the book is six self-guided walks and tours that zero in on Paris' greatest sights and neighborhoods. The Historic Paris Walk takes you through the heart of the city—soaring Notre-Dame, the bustling Latin Quarter, and the stained-glass wonder of Sainte-Chapelle. You'll see all the essentials of the vast Louvre and Orsay museums, while still leaving time for browsing. Ascend the 1,000-foot Eiffel Tower at sunset and watch the City of Light light up. Stroll Rue Cler's friendly (and odiferous) shops, and take a side-trip to Versailles for chandeliered palaces and manicured gardens.

The rest of the book is a traveler's tool kit. You'll find plenty more about Paris' attractions, from shopping to nightlife to less touristy sights. And there are helpful hints on saving money, avoiding crowds, getting around on the Métro, finding a great meal, and much more.

If you'd like more information than this Pocket Guide offers, I've sprinkled the book liberally with web references. For general travel tips—as well as updates for this book—see ricksteves.com.

Key to This Book

Sights are rated:

▲▲▲ **Don't miss**
▲▲ **Try hard to see**
▲ **Worthwhile if you can make it**
No rating **Worth knowing about**

Tourist information offices are abbreviated as **TI**, bathrooms are **WCs**, and Métro stops are **Mo.**

Like Europe, this book uses the **24-hour clock.** It's the same through 12:00 noon, then keep going: 13:00 (1:00 p.m.), 14:00 (2:00 p.m.), and so on.

For opening times, if a sight is listed as "May-Oct daily 9:00-16:00," it's open from 9 a.m. until 4 p.m. from the first day of May until the last day of October.

Paris by Neighborhood

Central Paris (population 2.2 million) is circled by a ring-road, and split in half by the Seine River, which runs east–west. If you were on a boat floating downstream, the Right Bank would be on your right, and the Left Bank on your left. The bull's-eye on your map is Notre-Dame, on an island in the middle of the Seine.

Twenty arrondissements (administrative districts) spiral out from the center, like an escargot shell. If your hotel's zip code is 75007, you know (from the last two digits) that it's in the 7th arrondissement. The city is speckled with Métro stops, and most Parisians locate addresses by the closest stop nearby. So in Parisian jargon, the Eiffel Tower is on *la Rive Gauche* (the Left Bank) in the *7ème* (7th arrondissement), zip code 75007, Mo: Trocadéro (the closest Métro stop).

Think of Paris as a series of neighborhoods, cradling major landmarks.

The Historic Core: Paris got its start around Notre-Dame, on the Île

Paris' Neighborhoods

PERIPHERIQUE (RING FREEWAY)

MONTMARTRE

ARC DE
TRIOMPHE

CHAMPS-
ELYSEES

LOUVRE

MAJOR
MUSEUMS

ORSAY

POMPIDOU
MUSEUM

MARAIS

NOTRE-
DAME

PLACE
DES VOSGES

HISTORIC
CORE

RUE
CLER

LEFT BANK

PERE
LACHAISE
CEMETERY

EIFFEL
TOWER

ARMY
MUSEUM

LUXEMBOURG
GARDEN

Seine

River

Introduction

Daily Reminder

Sunday: Many sights are free on the first Sunday of the month, includ-ing the Louvre, Orsay, Rodin, and Cluny museums, the Arc de Triomphe (Oct-March only), and Pompidou Center. These free days at popular sights attract hordes of visitors. Versailles is more crowded than usual on Sunday—but on the upside, the garden's fountains are running (April-Oct).

Look for organ concerts at St. Sulpice and possibly other churches. The American Church often has classical piano concerts June-Sept at 17:00 (near the Eiffel Tower, 65 Quai d'Orsay, acparis.org). Summer brings puppet shows to Luxembourg Garden and the Champ de Mars park. Most of Paris' stores are closed on Sunday, but shoppers will find shopping opportunities along the Champs-Elysées, at flea markets, and in the Marais neighborhood. Many recommended restaurants in the Rue Cler neighborhood are closed for dinner.

Monday: These sights are closed today: Orsay, Rodin, Marmottan, Carnavalet, Catacombs, Petit Palais, Victor Hugo's House, Deportation Memorial, Archaeological Crypt, and the sights at Versailles. The Louvre is more crowded because of these closings. Off-season, the Army Museum and Napoleon's Tomb are closed the first Monday of the month. Market streets such as Rue Cler and Rue Mouffetard are dead today. Some banks are closed. It's discount night at many cinemas.

Tuesday: Many sights are closed today, including the Louvre,

de la Cité ("Island of the City"). There you'll find Paris' oldest sights, from Roman ruins to the medieval Sainte-Chapelle church.

The Major Museums: To the west, the Louvre, Orsay, and Orangerie museums cluster around the fringes of the Tuileries Garden.

The Champs-Elysées: The greatest 19th-century boulevard—stretching two miles from the Tuileries to the Arc de Triomphe—anchors a neighborhood of grand Right Bank sights, including the Opéra Garnier.

Eiffel Tower neighborhood: In the Tower's shadow lies colorful Rue Cler, with its village-like market and recommended hotels and restaurants.

Orangerie, Cluny, and Pompidou museums. The Orsay and Versailles are particularly busy. The gardens at Versailles have music and/or fountain displays in summer (check hours). Napoleon's Tomb and the "Louis XIV" wing of the Army Museum are open until 21:00 (April-Sept).

Wednesday: All sights are open, and some have late hours, including the Louvre (until 21:45, last entry 21:00), the Rodin Museum (until 20:45), and Sainte-Chapelle (until 21:30 mid-May-mid-Sept). The weekly *Pariscope* magazine comes out today. Most schools are closed, so many kids' sights are busy.

Thursday: All sights are open except the Sewer Tour. Some sights are open late, including the Orsay (until 21:45, last entry 21:00) and Marmottan (20:00). Some department stores are open late.

Friday: All sights are open except the Sewer Tour. The Louvre stays open until 21:45 (last entry 21:00) and Notre-Dame's tower until 23:00 (July-Aug). Afternoon trains and roads leaving Paris are crowded. Restaurants are busy—it's smart to book ahead.

Saturday: All sights are open except the Jewish Art and History Museum. The fountains run at Versailles April-Oct (nice but very crowded). Notre-Dame's tower is open until 23:00 (July-Aug), and the Picasso Museum may be open until 22:00. Department stores are jammed. In summer, puppet shows are held at Luxembourg Garden and the Champ de Mars park. Restaurants are busy—reserve ahead.

Sights include the Rodin Museum and the Army Museum and Napoleon's Tomb.

The Left Bank: Between the river and the Luxembourg Garden, the Left Bank is known for Paris' intellectual, artistic, and café life. It's also one of Paris' best boutique shopping areas.

The Marais: Stretching from the Pompidou Center to Place Bastille, this neighborhood is the upwardly mobile Paris of today—with trendy restaurants, shops, nightlife, and artistic sights such as the Pompidou Center and Picasso Museum.

Paris at a Glance

Introduction

▲▲▲**Notre-Dame Cathedral** Paris' most beloved church, with towers and gargoyles. **Hours:** Cathedral Mon-Fri 7:45-18:45, Sat-Sun 8:00-19:15; tower daily April-Sept 10:00-18:30, Fri-Sat until 23:00 in July-Aug, Oct-March 10:00-17:30. See page 17.

▲▲▲**Sainte-Chapelle** Gothic cathedral with peerless stained glass. **Hours:** March-Oct daily 9:30-18:00, Wed until 21:30 mid-May-mid-Sept, Nov-Feb daily 9:00-17:00. See page 34.

▲▲▲**Louvre** Europe's oldest and greatest museum, starring *Mona Lisa* and *Venus de Milo*. **Hours:** Wed-Mon 9:00-18:00, Wed and Fri until 21:45, closed Tue. See page 43.

▲▲▲**Orsay Museum** Nineteenth-century art, including Europe's greatest Impressionist collection. **Hours:** Tue-Sun 9:30-18:00, Thu until 21:45, closed Mon. See page 69.

▲▲▲**Eiffel Tower** Paris' soaring exclamation point. **Hours:** Daily mid-June-Aug 9:00-24:45, Sept-mid-June 9:30-23:45. See page 99.

▲▲▲**Champs-Elysées** Paris' grand boulevard. **Hours:** Always open. See page 160.

▲▲▲**Versailles** The ultimate royal palace (Château), with a Hall of Mirrors, vast gardens, a grand canal, plus a queen's playground. **Hours:** Château April-Oct Tue-Sun 9:00-18:30, Nov-March Tue-Sun 9:00-17:30, closed Mon year-round. Trianon/Domaine de Marie-Antoinette April-Oct Tue-Sun 12:00-18:30, Nov-March Tue-Sun 12:00-17:30, closed Mon year-round; in winter only the two Trianon Palaces are open. Gardens open April-Oct daily 9:00-20:30, Nov-March Tue-Sun 8:00-18:00, closed Mon. See page 121.

▲▲**Orangerie Museum** Monet's water lilies, plus works by Utrillo, Cézanne, Renoir, Matisse, and Picasso, in a lovely setting. **Hours:** Wed-Mon 9:00-18:00, closed Tue. See page 149.

▲▲**Rodin Museum** Works by the greatest sculptor since Michelangelo, with many statues in a peaceful garden. **Hours:** Tue-Sun 10:00-17:45, Wed until 20:45, closed Mon. See page 151.

▲▲**Army Museum and Napoleon's Tomb** The emperor's imposing tomb, flanked by museums of France's wars. **Hours:** Museum daily April-Sept 10:00-18:00, "Louis XIV to Napoleon I" wing Tue until 21:00;

Oct-March 10:00-17:00, closed first Mon of month Oct-June. Tomb daily April-June and Sept 10:00-18:00, Tue until 21:00; July-Aug 10:00-19:00, some Tue until 21:00; Oct-March 10:00-17:00, closed first Mon of month Sept-May. See page 153.

▲▲**Marmottan Museum** Untouristy art museum focusing on Monet. **Hours:** Tue-Sun 10:00-18:00, Thu until 20:00, closed Mon. See page 154.

▲▲**Cluny Museum** Medieval art with unicorn tapestries. **Hours:** Wed-Mon 9:15-17:45, closed Tue. See page 157.

▲▲**Arc de Triomphe** Triumphal arch with viewpoint, marking start of Champs-Elysées. **Hours:** Interior daily April-Sept 10:00-23:00, Oct-March 10:00-22:30. See page 161.

▲▲**Jacquemart-André Museum** Art-strewn mansion. **Hours:** Daily 10:00-18:00, Mon and Sat until 20:30 for special exhibits. See page 164.

▲▲**Picasso Museum** World's largest collection of Picasso's works. **Hours:** Daily 9:00-19:30, some Sat until 22:00. See page 167.

▲▲**Pompidou Center** Modern art in colorful building with city views. **Hours:** Wed-Mon 11:00-21:00, closed Tue. See page 166.

▲▲**Sacré-Cœur and Montmartre** White basilica atop Montmartre with spectacular views. **Hours:** Daily 6:00-22:30; dome climb daily May-Sept 9:00-19:00, Oct-April 9:00-17:00. See page 169.

▲**Panthéon** Neoclassical monument celebrating the struggles of the French. **Hours:** Daily 10:00-18:30 in summer, until 18:00 in winter. See page 158.

▲**Opéra Garnier** Grand belle époque theater with a modern ceiling by Chagall. **Hours:** Generally daily 10:00-16:30, mid-July-Aug until 18:00. See page 162.

▲**Carnavalet Museum** Paris' history wrapped up in a 16th-century mansion. **Hours:** Tue-Sun 10:00-18:00, closed Mon. See page 168.

▲**Jewish Art and History Museum** Displays history of Judaism in Europe. **Hours:** Sun-Fri 11:00-18:00, closed Sat. See page 167.

▲**Père Lachaise Cemetery** Final home of Paris' illustrious dead. **Hours:** Mon-Fri 8:00-18:00, Sat 8:30-18:00, Sun 9:00-18:00, closes at 17:30 in winter. See page 169.

Montmartre: This hill, topped by the bulbous white domes of Sacré-Cœur, hovers on the northern fringes of your Paris map. The neighborhood still retains some of the untamed rural charm that once drew Impressionist painters and turn-of-the-century bohemians.

Planning Your Time

The following day-plans give an idea of how much an organized, motivated, and caffeinated person can see. Trying to do too much would drive you in-Seine, so leave a few things for your next visit to Paris. Paris is a great one-week getaway. If you have less than a week, start with the Day 1 plan—the most important sights—and add on from there.

Day 1: Follow this book's Historic Paris Walk. In the afternoon, tour the Louvre. Then enjoy the Trocadéro scene and a twilight ride up the Eiffel Tower.

Day 2: Stroll the Champs-Elysées from the Arc de Triomphe to the Tuileries Garden. Tour the Orsay Museum. In the evening, take a nighttime tour by cruise boat, taxi, bus, or retro-chic Deux Chevaux car.

Day 3: Catch the RER suburban train by 8:00 to arrive early at Versailles. Tour the palace's interior. Then either tour the gardens or return to Paris for more sightseeing.

Day 4: Visit Montmartre and the Sacré-Cœur Basilica. Have lunch on Montmartre. Continue your Impressionist theme by touring the Orangerie. Enjoy dinner on Ile St. Louis, then a floodlit walk by Notre-Dame.

Day 5: Concentrate on the morning market in the Rue Cler neighborhood, then afternoon sightseeing at the Rodin Museum and the Army Museum and Napoleon's Tomb.

Day 6: Ride scenic bus #69 to the Marais and tour this neighborhood, including the Pompidou Center. In the afternoon, visit the Opéra

Garnier, and end your day with rooftop views from the Galeries Lafayette or Printemps department stores.

Day 7: See more in Paris (Rue Montorgueil market, Left Bank shopping stroll, Père Lachaise Cemetery, Marmottan or Jacquemart-André museum), or take a day-trip to Chartres or Giverny.

These are busy day-plans, so be sure to schedule in slack time for picnics, laundry, people-watching, leisurely dinners, shopping, and re-charging your touristic batteries. Slow down and be open to unexpected experiences and the courtesy of Parisians.

Quick Tips: Here are a few quick sightseeing tips to get you started—for more on these topics and other ideas, ✪ see page 207. Consider the handy Paris Museum Pass, which covers admission to many sights and lets you skip ticket-buying lines. Reservations are recommended for the Eiffel Tower (book early). Since opening hours are variable, get the latest information from museum websites, at parisinfo.com, or from local publications when you arrive. Take advantage of my free Paris audio tours, covering many of this book's sights.

And finally, remember that—although Paris' sights can be crowded and stressful—the city itself is all about gentility and grace, so...be flexible.

I hope you have a great trip! Traveling like a temporary local, you'll get the absolute most out of every mile, minute, and euro. As you visit places I know and love, I'm happy you'll be meeting my favorite Parisians.

Bon voyage!

Historic Paris Walk

Ile de la Cité and the Latin Quarter

Paris has been the cultural capital of Europe for centuries. We'll start where it did, on Ile de la Cité, with a foray onto the Left Bank, on a walk that laces together 80 generations of history—from Celtic fishing village to Roman city, bustling medieval capital, birthplace of the Revolution, bohemian haunt of the 1920s, and the working world of modern Paris. Along the way, we'll step into two of Paris' greatest sights: Notre-Dame and Sainte-Chapelle.

Allow a good four hours for this three-mile walk, including time inside the sights. Allow a little more time to pause for lunch or a *café crème,* to browse for antique books, or to watch the lazy flow of the timeless Seine.

ORIENTATION

Paris Museum Pass: Because several sights on this walk are covered by the pass, consider picking it up before your walk (or, on the Ile de la Cité, at the *tabac* by Sainte-Chapelle at 5 Boulevard du Palais). For details, ✪ see page 208.

Notre-Dame Cathedral: Free, open Mon-Fri 7:45-18:45, Sat-Sun 8:00-19:15. Modest dress expected. The cathedral hosts several masses (early morning, noon, and evening), plus Vespers at 17:45. For a schedule of services, organ concerts, and summer night spectacles, call or check the website. Tel. 01 42 34 56 10, notredamedeparis.fr.

Tower Climb: The entry for Notre-Dame's towers is outside the cathedral, on the left side. It's 400 steps up, but it's worth it for the gargoyle's-eye view of the cathedral, Seine, and city. It costs €8.50, and is covered by the Museum Pass, but there's no bypass line for passholders. Open April-Sept daily 10:00-18:30, Fri-Sat until 23:00 in July-Aug; Oct-March daily 10:00-17:30; last entry 45 minutes before closing. To avoid peak season crowds, arrive before 10:00 or after 17:00.

Paris Archaeological Crypt: €4, covered by Museum Pass, Tue-Sun 10:00-18:00, closed Mon, last entry 30 minutes before closing.

Deportation Memorial: Free, Tue-Sun April-Sept 10:00-19:00, Oct-March 10:00-17:00, closed Mon year-round, may randomly close.

Shakespeare and Company Bookstore: Mon-Fri 10:00-23:00, Sat-Sun 11:00-23:00; tel. 01 43 25 40 93.

Sainte-Chapelle: €8.50, €12.50 combo-ticket with Conciergerie, covered by Museum Pass. Open March-Oct daily 9:30-18:00, Wed until 21:30 mid-May-mid-Sept; Nov-Feb daily 9:00-17:00; last entry 30 minutes before closing. Avoid the ticket line with a Museum Pass or a combo-ticket bought at the Conciergerie. Security is strict at the entrance. No one can skip to the front of the security line (though you could flash your pass and try). To minimize the wait, arrive before opening or visit late.

Conciergerie: €8.50, €12.50 combo-ticket with Sainte-Chapelle, covered by Museum Pass. Open daily 9:30-18:00, last entry 30 minutes before closing. Tel. 01 53 40 60 80.

Audio Tour: You can download this chapter as a free Rick Steves **audio tour** (✪ see page 207).

WCs: At Notre-Dame (free), Sainte-Chapelle, the Conciergerie, and cafés.

THE WALK BEGINS

Start at Notre-Dame Cathedral on the island in the Seine River, the physical and historic bull's-eye of your Paris map. The closest Métro stops are Cité, Hôtel de Ville, and St. Michel, each a short walk away.

▶ *On the square in front of the cathedral, stand far enough back to take in the whole facade. Find the circular window in the center.*

Notre-Dame Cathedral

For centuries, the main figure in the Christian pantheon has been Mary, the mother of Jesus. This church is dedicated to "Our Lady" *(Notre Dame),* and there she is, cradling God, right in the heart of the facade, surrounded by the halo of the rose window.

Imagine the faith of the people who built this cathedral. They broke ground in 1163 with the hope that someday their great-great-great-great-great-great grandchildren might attend the dedication Mass, which finally took place two centuries later, in 1345. Look up the 200-foot-tall bell towers and imagine a tiny medieval community mustering the money and energy for construction. Master masons supervised, but the people did much of the grunt work themselves for free—hauling the huge stones from distant quarries, digging a 30-foot-deep trench to lay the foundation, and treading like rats on a wheel designed to lift the stones up, one by one. This kind of backbreaking, arduous manual labor created the real hunchbacks of Notre-Dame.

▶ *"Walk this way" toward the cathedral, and view it from the bronze plaque on the ground (30 yards from the central doorway) marked...*

Notre-Dame—a 200-year construction project

Rose window framing "Our Lady"

Historic Paris Walk

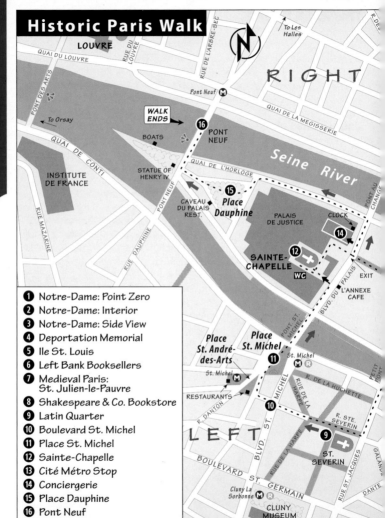

Historic Paris Walk

LOUVRE

QUAI DU LOUVRE

RUE DU LOUVRE

R. DE L'ARBRE-SEC

R. DE...

To Les Halles

RIGHT

PONT DES ARTS

To Orsay

QUAI DE CONTI

Pont Neuf Ⓜ

QUAI DE LA MEGISSERIE

WALK ENDS

Ⓖ 16

BOATS

PONT NEUF

Seine River

STATUE OF HENRY IV

QUAI DE L'HORLOGE

INSTITUTE DE FRANCE

PONT NEUF

CAVEAU DU PALAIS REST.

Ⓖ 15 Place Dauphine

PALAIS DE JUSTICE

CLOCK

Ⓖ 14

RUE DAUPHINE

RUE MAZARINE

PONT AU CHANGE

SAINTE-CHAPELLE

Ⓖ 12

WC

EXIT

L'ANNEXE CAFE

BLVD. DU PALAIS

Place St. André-des-Arts

Place St. Michel

PONT ST. MICHEL

Ⓖ 11 St. Michel Ⓜ Ⓡ

St. Michel Ⓜ

RESTAURANTS

Ⓖ 10

R. DANTON

BLVD. ST. MICHEL

R. DE LA HUCHETTE

RUE DE LA HARPE

PETIT PONT

RUE DE LA...

R. STE. SEVERIN

Ⓖ 9

ST. SEVERIN

RUE ST. JACQUES

GALANDE

DANTE

LEFT

BOULEVARD

ST. GERMAIN

Cluny La Sorbonne Ⓜ Ⓡ

CLUNY MUSEUM

❶ Notre-Dame: Point Zero
❷ Notre-Dame: Interior
❸ Notre-Dame: Side View
❹ Deportation Memorial
❺ Ile St. Louis
❻ Left Bank Booksellers
❼ Medieval Paris: St. Julien-le-Pauvre
❽ Shakespeare & Co. Bookstore
❾ Latin Quarter
❿ Boulevard St. Michel
⓫ Place St. Michel
⓬ Sainte-Chapelle
⓭ Cité Métro Stop
⓮ Conciergerie
⓯ Place Dauphine
⓰ Pont Neuf

POMPIDOU
CENTER

HOMAGE TO
STRAVINSKY
FOUNTAIN

RUE BLANCS MANTEAUX

RUE DU TEMPLE

RUE STE. CROIX DE LA BRETTONERIE

PLÂTRE

RUE DES ARCHIVES

ST.
MERRI

RUE QUINCAMPOIX

BLVD. DE SEBASTOPOL

HALLES

RUE DE RIVOLI

TOUR
ST. JACQUES

RUE DU RENARD

BANK

RUE DE MOUSSY

M Châtelet

Place
du Châtelet

MARAIS

QUAI DE GESVRES

QUAI DE L'HOTEL DE VILLE

M
Hôtel
de Ville

HOTEL
DE VILLE

RUE DE RIVOLI

PONT NOTRE DAME

To Place de
la Bastille

RUE FRANÇOIS MIRON

QUAI DE LA CORSE

R. BARRES

R. LOUIS PHILIPPE

Flower
Market

M Cité

RUE DE
LUTÈCE

Ile de
la Cité

PONT D'ARCOLE

ST.
GERVAIS

HOLOCAUST
MEMORIAL

QUAI DES CELE(S)INS

B

RUE DE LA CITÉ

R St. Michel

ARCHAEO-
LOGICAL
CRYPT

AU BOUDINANTE
RESTAURANT

RUE CHANOINESSE

VOIE GEORGES POMPIDOU

GOOD
PICNIC SPOT

PONT LOUIS PHILIPPE

Place du
Parvis ❶

👣 WALK
BEGINS

TOWER
ENTRANCE

To Pont Marie M

CHARLEMAGNE
STATUE

WC

❷

NOTRE-
DAME

QUAI DE BOURBON

❺

PONT
MARIE

❽

❸

PONT
ST. LOUIS

RUE ST. LOUIS-EN-L'ILE

Ile
St. Louis

PONT AU DOUBLE

GROCERY
STORE

CAFE
MED

POST

❼ Square
Viviani

B

QUAI DE MONTEBELLO

❻

QUAI D'ORLEANS

AMORINI
GELATI

BAKERY

RUE LA GRANGE

RESTAURANTS
ON BARGES

▲❹

BERTHILLON
ICE CREAM

ST.
LOUIS

BANK

PONT DE L'ARCHEVECHE

QUAI DE LA
TOURNELLE

200 Meters

200 Yards

PONT
TOURNELLE

QUAI DE
BETHUNE

❶ Point Zero

You're standing at the center of France, the point from which all distances are measured. It was also the center of Paris 2,300 years ago, when the Parisii tribe fished where the east–west river crossed a north–south road. The Romans conquered this Celtic tribe and built their Temple of Jupiter where Notre-Dame stands today (52 B.C.). When Rome fell, the Germanic Franks sealed their victory by replacing the temple with the Christian church of St. Etienne in the sixth century.

The grand equestrian statue (to your right, as you face the church) is of Charlemagne ("Charles the Great," 742-814), King of the Franks, whose reign marked the birth of modern France.

When Notre-Dame was first built, this square was filled with higgledy-piggledy buildings. The church's huge bell towers rose above this tangle of smaller buildings, inspiring Victor Hugo's story of a deformed bell-ringer who could look down on all of Paris. Looking two-thirds of the way up Notre-Dame's left tower, find Paris' most photographed gargoyle. Propped on his elbows on the balcony rail, he watches all the tourists in line.

▶ *Much of Paris' history is right under your feet. Some may consider visiting it in the Archaeological Crypt, a small museum located 100 yards in front of Notre-Dame. Otherwise, turn your attention to the...*

Notre-Dame Facade

▶ *Start with the left doorway and, to the left of the door, find the statue of St. Denis, with his head in his hands.*

Left Door—St. Denis: When Christianity began making converts in Roman Paris, the bishop of Paris, Denis, was beheaded by the Romans.

Point Zero: Step on the center of France.

Charlemagne, whose "Franks" became "France"

Paris Through History

250 B.C.	Small fishing village of the Parisii, a Celtic tribe.
52 B.C.	Julius Caesar conquers the Parisii, and the Romans soon establish a capital on the Left Bank.
A.D. 497	Roman Paris falls to the Germanic Franks. King Clovis (482-511) converts to Christianity and makes Paris his capital.
885-886	Paris gets wasted in a siege by Viking Norsemen = Normans.
1163	Notre-Dame cornerstone laid.
c. 1250	Paris is a bustling commercial city with a newly built university, Notre-Dame, and Sainte-Chapelle.
c. 1600	King Henry IV beautifies Paris with structures such as the Pont Neuf.
c. 1700	Louis XIV makes Versailles his capital. Parisians grumble.
1789	Paris is the heart of France's Revolution, which condemns thousands to the guillotine.
1804	Napoleon Bonaparte crowns himself emperor in a ceremony at Notre-Dame.
c. 1860	Napoleon's nephew, Napoleon III, builds Paris' wide boulevards.
1889	The centennial of the Revolution is celebrated with the Eiffel Tower. Paris enjoys the prosperity of the belle époque (beautiful age).
1920s	After the draining Great War, Paris is a cheap place to live, attracting expatriates such as Ernest Hemingway.
1940-1944	Occupied Paris spends the war years under gray skies and gray Nazi uniforms.
1968	Student protests and a general strike bring Paris to a halt.
1981-1995	Paris modernizes: the TGV, the new Louvre Pyramid, Musée d'Orsay, La Grande Arche de la Défense, and Opéra Bastille.
1998	Playing at its home stadium, France wins the World Cup.
2014	With its Autolib' rent-a-car system, Vélib' bikes, and traffic-free riverside zones, Paris is a global leader in greenification.

But those early Christians were hard to keep down. Denis simply got up, tucked his head under his arm, "headed" north, paused at a fountain to wash it off, and continued until he found just the right place to meet his maker. Christianity gained ground, and a church soon replaced the pagan temple.

Central Door—Last Judgment Relief: Above the doorway (just under the arches), witness the end of the world. Christ sits on the throne of judgment holding both hands up. Beneath him an angel and a demon weigh souls in the balance; the demon cheats by pressing down. The good souls stand to the left, gazing up to heaven. The bad souls to the right are chained up and led off to a six-hour tour of the Louvre on a hot summer day.

Above the Doors—The Kings of Judah: In the days of the French Revolution (1789-1799), this row of 28 biblical kings was mistaken for the hated French kings. The citizens stormed the church, crying, "Off with their heads!" Plop—they lopped off the crowned heads of these statues with glee, creating a row of St. Denises that wasn't repaired for decades. But the story doesn't end there. A schoolteacher collected the heads and buried them in his backyard for safekeeping. There they slept until 1977, when they were accidentally unearthed. Today, they're on display in the Cluny Museum, a few blocks away (✪ see page 157).

▶ *Let's go inside. Enter the church at the right doorway and find a spot where you can view the long, high central nave. (Be careful: Pickpockets attend church here religiously.)*

❷ Notre-Dame Interior: The Nave

Remove your metaphorical hat and become a simple bareheaded

St. Denis with head in hands

Last Judgment (over the central door)

Notre-Dame Facade

"WOW—WHAT A GREAT VIEW!"

ENTHRALLED TOURISTS

BORED GARGOYLE

GARGOYLES

MARY IN ROSE WINDOW

28 KINGS OF JUDAH

ST. DENIS (HOLDING HIS HEAD)

PORTAL OF MARY

LAST JUDGMENT

PORTAL OF ST. ANNE

Seine River

To Left Bank & Latin Quarter

To Right Bank

TOWER ENTRANCE

EXIT

ENTER

To View Of Flying Buttresses & Deportation Memorial

PONT AU DOUBLE

DRINKING FOUNTAIN

HOTEL DIEU

POINT ZERO

WC

CHARLEMAGNE STATUE

Place du Parvis

To Sainte-Chapelle

To Archaeological Crypt & Place St. Michel

peasant, entering the dim medieval light of the church. Take a minute to let your pupils dilate, then take in the subtle, mysterious light show that God beams through the stained-glass windows. Follow the slender columns up 10 stories to the praying-hands arches of the ceiling, and contemplate the heavens.

This is Gothic. Taller and filled with light, Notre-Dame was a major improvement over the earlier Romanesque style. Gothic architects needed only a few structural columns, topped by crisscrossing pointed arches, to

Notre-Dame's soaring Gothic arches

Pietà behind the altar

support the weight of the roof. This let them build higher than ever, freeing up the walls for windows.

Notre-Dame has the typical basilica floor plan: a long central nave lined with columns and flanked by side aisles. It's designed in the shape of a cross, with the altar placed where the crossbeam intersects. The church can hold up to 10,000 faithful. It's probably buzzing with visitors now, just as it was centuries ago, when churches were the busy center of every community.

▶ Walk up to the main altar.

Altar

This marks the place where Mass is said and the bread and wine of Communion are blessed and distributed. In olden days, there were no chairs. This was the holy spot for Romans, Christians...and even atheists during the Revolution. France today, though nominally Catholic, remains aloof from Vatican dogmatism. Instead of traditional wooden confessional booths, there's an inviting **glass-walled room** (right aisle), where modern sinners seek counseling as much as forgiveness.

Just past the altar is the so-called "choir," the area enclosed with carved-wood walls, where more intimate services can be held in this spacious building. At the far end of the choir (under the cross) is a fine **17th-century *pietà*** flanked by a kneeling King Louis XIV (1638-1715) and his less-famous father.

In the right transept is a statue of **Joan of Arc** (Jeanne d'Arc, 1412-1431), dressed in armor and praying. The statue honors the French teenager who rallied her country's soldiers to try to drive English invaders from Paris. The English and their allies burned her at the stake for claiming to

Notre-Dame Interior

1 View of Nave
2 Glass-Walled Confessional Room
3 Pietà Flanked by Louis XIII & Louis XIV
4 Joan of Arc Statue
5 Rose-Shaped Window
6 Thomas Aquinas Painting
7 Scenes of the Resurrected Jesus

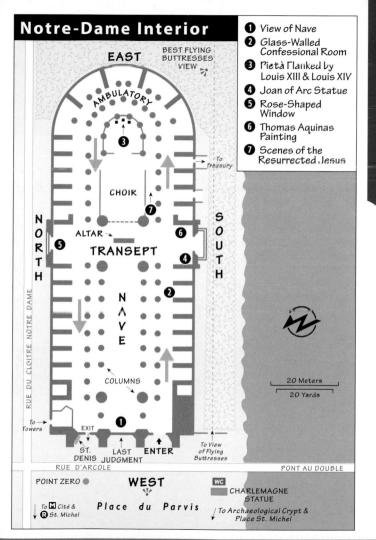

EAST

BEST FLYING BUTTRESSES VIEW

AMBULATORY

To Treasury

CHOIR

3

7

NORTH

ALTAR

5

TRANSEPT

6

4

SOUTH

RUE DU CLOÎTRE NOTRE DAME

N
A
V
E

2

COLUMNS

20 Meters
20 Yards

To Towers

EXIT

ST. DENIS

LAST JUDGMENT

ENTER

To View of Flying Buttresses

RUE D'ARCOLE

PONT AU DOUBLE

POINT ZERO

WEST

WC

CHARLEMAGNE STATUE

To Cité & St. Michel

Place du Parvis

To Archaeological Crypt & Place St. Michel

Joan of Arc—former heretic, now saint

Original rose window in north transept

hear heavenly voices. Almost immediately, Parisians rallied to condemn Joan's execution, and finally, in 1909, here in Notre-Dame, the former "witch" was beatified.

Join the statue in gazing up to the blue-and-purple, **rose-shaped window** in the opposite transept, still with its original medieval glass.

A large painting back down to your right shows portly **Thomas Aquinas** (1225-1274) teaching, while his students drink from the fountain of knowledge. This Italian monk taught at the multicultural University of Paris, while he wrote "scholastic" theological works—using Aristotle's logic to examine the Christian universe, aiming to fuse faith and reason.

▶ *Continue toward the far end of the church.*

Circling the Choir

The back side of the choir walls feature **scenes of the resurrected Jesus** (c. 1350) appearing to his followers, starting with Mary Magdalene. The nearby **Treasury** contains lavish robes, golden reliquaries, and the humble tunic of King (and St.) Louis IX, but it probably isn't worth the €4 entry fee.

Surrounding the choir are chapels, each dedicated to a particular saint. One chapel displays a model showing how the medieval church was built—with pulleys, wagons, hamster-wheel cranes, and lots of elbow grease. At other chapels, the faithful can pause to light a candle as an offering, and meditate in the cool light of the stained glass.

▶ *Amble around the ambulatory, continuing to the exit. Spill back outside into the light of day, and make a slow U-turn left. Enter the park (recently renamed "Square Jean XXIII") through the iron gates along the riverside.*

Notre-Dame's gargoyles—hideous yet functional—can be seen up close if you climb the tower.

❸ Notre-Dame Side View

Alongside the church you'll notice the flying buttresses. These 50-foot stone beams that stick out of the church were the key to the complex Gothic architecture. The pointed arches we saw inside cause the weight of the roof to push outward rather than downward. The "flying" buttresses support the roof by pushing back inward. This opens up the walls for stained-glass windows.

The gargoyles at the base of the roof stick out from pillars and buttresses, representing souls caught between heaven and earth. They also function as rainspouts—from the same French root word as "gargle."

The Neo-Gothic 300-foot spire is a product of the 1860 reconstruction of the dilapidated old church. Find the restoration's chief architect, Eugène-Emmanuel Viollet-le-Duc, among the statues at the base of the spire, looking up, admiring his fine work.

It takes 13 tourists to build a Gothic church: one steeple, six columns, and six buttresses.

▶ *Behind Notre-Dame, cross the street and enter the park at the tip of the island. Look for the stairs that head down to the...*

❹ Deportation Memorial (Mémorial de la Déportation)

This memorial to the 200,000 French victims of the Nazi concentration camps (1940-1945) draws you into their experience. France was quickly overrun by Nazi Germany, and Paris spent the war years under Nazi occupation. Jews and dissidents were rounded up and deported—many never returned.

As you descend the steps, the city around you disappears. Surrounded by walls, you have become a prisoner. Inside, the hallway is lined with 200,000 lighted crystals, one for each French citizen who died. Flickering at the far end is the eternal flame of hope. Above the exit as you leave is the message you'll find at other Holocaust sites: "Forgive, but never forget."

▶ *Back on street level, look across the river (north) to the island called...*

❺ Ile St. Louis

If the Ile de la Cité is a tugboat laden with the history of Paris, it's towing this classy little residential dinghy, laden only with high-rent apartments, boutiques, and characteristic restaurants. The Ile is renowned for its ice-cream shops. Berthillon has outlets at 31 Rue St. Louis-en-l'Ile, another across the street, and a third around the corner on Rue Bellay. Gelato-lovers head instead to Amorino Gelati at 47 Rue St. Louis-en-l'Ile.

▶ *From the Deportation Memorial, cross the bridge onto the Left Bank and turn right (west). Walk along the river, toward the front end of Notre-Dame. This view of the church is one of Europe's classic sights.*

Deportation Memorial's 200,000 points of light

Booksellers line the Seine River.

LEFT BANK

❻ Left Bank Booksellers

The Rive Gauche, or the Left Bank of the Seine—"left" if you were floating downstream—still has many of the twisting lanes and narrow buildings of medieval times. The Right Bank is more modern and business-oriented, with wide boulevards and stressed Parisians in suits. Here along the riverbank, the "big business" is secondhand books, displayed in the green metal stalls on the parapet. With flexible hours and (literally) no overhead, these literary entrepreneurs—called *bouquinistes* (boo-keen-eest)—run their businesses as they have since the mid 1500s. Today, the waiting list to become one of Paris' 250 *bouquinistes* is eight years. Each *bouquiniste* is allowed four boxes, with rent around €100 per year.

▶ *When you reach the bridge (Pont au Double) that crosses over in front of Notre-Dame, veer to the left across the street to a small park called Square Viviani (fill your water bottle from the fountain on the left).*

Angle across the square and pass by Paris' oldest inhabitant—an acacia tree nicknamed Robinier, after the guy who planted it in 1602. Imagine that this same tree might once have shaded the Sun King, Louis XIV. Just beyond the tree you'll find the small rough-stone church of St. Julien-le-Pauvre.

❼ Medieval Paris (1000-1400)

Picture Paris in 1250, when the church of St. Julien-le-Pauvre was still new. Notre-Dame was nearly done (so they thought), Sainte-Chapelle had just opened, the university was expanding human knowledge, and Paris was fast becoming a prosperous industrial and commercial center. The area around the church (and along nearby Rue Galande) gives you some of the medieval feel of ramshackle architecture and old houses leaning every which way. In medieval days, people were piled on top of each other, here along the main commercial artery of the day—the Seine. The smell of fish competed with the smell of neighbors in this knot of humanity.

▶ *Return to the river and turn left, to #37 Rue de la Bûcherie...*

❽ Shakespeare and Company Bookstore

In addition to hosting butchers and fishmongers, the Left Bank has been home to scholars, philosophers, and poets since medieval times. This funky bookstore—a reincarnation of the original shop from the 1920s on Rue de l'Odéon—has picked up the literary torch.

Sylvia Beach, an American with a passion for free thinking, opened Shakespeare and Company for the post-WWI Lost Generation, who came to Paris to find themselves. American expatriates flocked here for the cheap rent and free-flowing booze, fleeing the uptight, Prohibition-era United States. Beach's bookstore was a meeting place for the likes of Ernest Hemingway, Gertrude Stein, and Ezra Pound. James Joyce struggled to find a publisher for his now-classic novel *Ulysses*—until Sylvia Beach published it.

▶ *Continue to Rue du Petit-Pont (which becomes Rue St. Jacques), and turn left. This bustling north–south boulevard was the Romans' busiest street 2,000 years ago, with chariots racing in and out of the city.*

A block south of the Seine, turn right at the Gothic church of St. Séverin and walk into the Latin Quarter.

St. Julien-le-Pauvre and 400-year-old tree

This bookstore carries on expatriate bohemian life.

St. Séverin flickers with flamboyant flames.

The Latin Quarter looks "Greek" today.

❾ Latin Quarter

As you walk alongside **St. Séverin church,** notice its Flamboyant, or "flame-like," Gothic architecture. The prickly spires are meant to make this building flicker in the eyes of the faithful. The gargoyles were decorative drain spouts that also functioned to keep evil spirits away. At **#22 Rue St. Séverin,** you'll find the skinniest house in Paris, two windows wide.

Although it may look more like the Greek Quarter today (cheap gyros abound), this area is the Latin Quarter, named for the language you'd have heard on these streets in medieval times. Latin-speaking scholars from across Europe gathered at the University of Paris (founded 1215), one of Europe's first universities, which was (and still is) nearby.

Notice how Rue St. Séverin's pavement slopes into a central channel of bricks. In the days before plumbing and toilets, flushing meant throwing it out the window. *"Garde de l'eau!"* they'd holler, "Watch out for the water!" and heave it into the streets, where it would eventually wash down into the Seine. (Even today, you'll see water flowing along the gutters of many Parisian streets—the city's way of keeping Paris clean.)

Until the 19th century, all of Paris was like this—a medieval tangle of small streets. The ethnic feel of this area is nothing new, as it's been a melting pot and university district for almost 800 years.

▶ *Keep wandering straight, and you'll come to...*

❿ Boulevard St. Michel

Busy Boulevard St. Michel (or "boul' Miche") is the main artery for the Latin Quarter, culminating a block away (to the left) at the intersection with Boulevard St. Germain. There's still a bohemian vibe at cafés and

Eateries Along This Walk

The following spots make for a nice lunch or snack break (★ find them on the map on page 18).

Au Bougnante: Local hangout a mere block north of Notre-Dame, where cops and workers get sandwiches, coffee, and €15 *formules* (a.k.a., two-course *menus;* 26 Rue Chanoinesse).

Ile St. Louis: Stop for gelato at renowned Berthillon (three locations along the main drag, original at 31 Rue St. Louis-en-l'Ile), or at Amorino Gelati (at #47), or for crêpes and a view at Café Med (★ see page 191).

Barges in the Seine: Sometimes docked near Notre-Dame are café-barges with stunning views.

Place St. André-des-Arts: Two nice outdoor restaurants sit amid the bustle on this tree-filled square near Place St. Michel.

L'Annexe Café: Coffee shop is conveniently located across from Sainte-Chapelle's entrance.

Caveau du Palais: Relaxing restaurant rest stop in leafy Place Dauphine.

boutiques nearby, although nowadays you're more likely to find pantyhose at 30 percent off.

The Sorbonne—the University of Paris' humanities department—is two blocks south, if you want to make a detour. (You can gaze at the dome from the Place de la Sorbonne courtyard, but visitors are not allowed to enter.) Founded as a theological school in medieval times, the Sorbonne expanded to include secular subjects and gained a worldwide reputation for bold new ideas. Nonconformity is still a tradition here, and Paris remains a world center for new intellectual trends.

▶ *Cross Boulevard St. Michel. Just ahead is a tiny tree-lined square called* **Place St. André-des-Arts.** *From there, turn right and enter the triangular Place St. Michel, with a Métro stop and a statue of St. Michael killing a devil.*

⑪ Place St. Michel

You're standing at the traditional core of the Left Bank's artsy, bohemian

Place St. Michel, where revolutionaries gather

Sainte-Chapelle—built for the Crown of Thorns

district of poets, philosophers, and winos. Nearby (especially west of the square along Rue St. André-des-Arts), you'll find international eateries, far-out bookshops, street singers, pale girls in black berets, jazz clubs, avant-garde cinemas, and—these days—tourists. The Left Bank's best action is after dark.

The neighborhood abounds with Paris' social watering holes: cafés. Every great French writer—from Voltaire and Jean-Jacques Rousseau to Jean-Paul Sartre and Jacques Derrida—had his favorite café, offering a warm place to sit and stimulating conversation for the price of a cup of coffee.

Place St. Michel has long been a gathering point for rebellion. In 1830, 1848, and again in 1871, the citizens took the streets from the government troops, set up barricades *Les Miz*-style, and fought against royalist oppression. During World War II, the locals rose up against their Nazi oppressors—read the plaques under the dragons at the foot of the St. Michel fountain. And in the spring of 1968, a time of social upheaval all over the world, young students battled riot batons and tear gas by digging up the cobblestones on the street and hurling them at police. They took over the square and declared it an independent state, forcing change. Demonstrations still take place here, but the Latin Quarter's cobblestones have been replaced with pavement, so scholars can never again use the streets as weapons.

▶ *From Place St. Michel, head north across the river toward the prickly steeple of the Sainte-Chapelle church. Along Boulevard du Palais, on your left, you'll see the doorway to Sainte-Chapelle.*

Security is strict and lines can be long at the Sainte-Chapelle complex because this is more than a tourist attraction: France's Supreme Court meets to the right of Sainte-Chapelle in the Palais de Justice. Once past security, you'll enter the church courtyard, with WCs and info on upcoming church concerts. Buy your Sainte-Chapelle ticket here, or—if you have a Museum Pass—you can bypass the ticket-buying line.

⑫ Sainte-Chapelle

This triumph of Gothic church architecture is a cathedral of glass like no other. It was speedily built between 1242 and 1248 for King Louis IX—the only French king who is now a saint—to house the supposed Crown of Thorns. Its architectural harmony is due to the fact that it was completed under the direction of one architect and in only six years—unheard of in Gothic times. Recall that Notre-Dame took over 200 years.

Though the inside is beautiful, the exterior is basically functional. The muscular buttresses hold up the stone roof, so the walls are essentially there to display stained glass. The lacy spire is Neo-Gothic—added in the 19th century.

▶ *Enter. First you see the relatively humble ground floor. Then climb the spiral staircase and step into the light.*

Interior: The Stained Glass

Fiat lux. "Let there be light." From the first page of the Bible, it's clear: Light is divine. Light shines through stained glass like God's grace shining down to earth. Gothic architects used their new technology to turn dark stone buildings into lanterns of light. The glory of Gothic shines brighter here than in any other church.

Fifteen separate panels of stained glass cover 6,500 square feet—two-thirds of it 13th-century original. There are more than 1,100 different scenes, mostly from the Bible. These tell the entire Christian history of the world, from the Creation in Genesis (first window on the left, as you face the altar), to the coming of Christ (over the altar), to the end of the world (the round "rose"-shaped window at the rear of the church). Each individual scene is interesting, and the whole effect is overwhelming. Allow yourself a few minutes to bask in the glow of the colored light, then zero in on some of the individual panels.

▶ *Working clockwise from the entrance, look for these worthwhile scenes. (Note: The sun lights up different windows at various times of day. Overcast days give the most even light. On bright, sunny days, some sections are glorious, while others look like sheets of lead.)*

Sainte-Chapelle

SOUVENIR SHOP & ANNEXE CAFÉ

To Notre-Dame & Latin Quarter

BLVD. DU PALAIS

EXIT

'JESUS' PASSION SCENES

ENTRANCE & SECURITY CHECK

WC

20 Meters

20 Yards

Sainte-Chapelle Courtyard

ALTAR

ST. LOUIS' PEEK-A-BOO WINDOW

CAMPAIGN OF HOLOFERNES

STAIRS

MORE MOSES

LIFE OF MOSES

BUTTRESSES

GENESIS SCENES

SPIRAL STAIRCASES

HELENA IN JERUSALEM

ROSE WINDOW

PALAIS DE JUSTICE (BUILDING SURROUNDS SAINTE-CHAPELLE)

BUTTRESSES
STAINED GLASS

ENTRANCE (INTO LOWER CHAPEL)

TICKETS

Genesis Scenes: The first window on the left starts the story. (Unfortunately, this window is always dark because of a building butted up against it.) On the bottom level in the third circle from the left, we see God create the round earth and hold it up.

Life of Moses (second window, the bottom row of diamond panels): The first panel shows baby Moses in a basket, placed by his sister in the squiggly brown river. Next he's found by the pharaoh's daughter. Then he grows up. And finally, he's a man, a prince of Egypt on his royal throne.

Ste.-Chapelle's crisscross arches and slim columns make the walls of stained glass possible.

Jesus' Passion Scenes (directly over the altar and behind the canopy): These scenes from Jesus' arrest and crucifixion were the backdrop for the Crown of Thorns, which was originally displayed on the altar. Find Jesus in yellow shorts, carrying his cross (fifth frame up from bottom right), and another scene (above the altar table) of Jesus in purple, being fitted with the painful Crown of Thorns.

Campaign of Holofernes (window to the right of the altar wall): On the bottom row are four scenes of colorful knights (refer to map to get oriented). The second circle from the left is a battle scene, the campaign of Holofernes. Three soldiers with swords are slaughtering three other men.

Notice the intricate details the glass-makers have created in this difficult medium. The background is blue. The men have different-colored clothes—red, blue, green, mauve, and white. You can see the folds in the robes, the hair, and facial features. The victim in the center has his head splotched with blood. Such details were created by scratching on the

Stained Glass Supreme

Craftsmen made glass—which is, essentially, melted sand—using this recipe:

- Melt one part sand with two parts wood ash.
- Mix in rusty metals to get different colors—iron makes red; cobalt makes blue; copper, green; manganese, purple; cadmium, yellow.
- Blow glass into a cylinder shape, cut lengthwise, and lay flat.
- Cut into pieces with an iron tool, or by heating and cooling a select spot to make it crack.
- Fit pieces together to form a figure, using strips of lead to hold them in place.
- Place masterpiece so high on a wall that no one can read it.

glass or baking on paint. It was a painstaking process of finding just the right colors, fitting them together to make a scene...and then multiplying by 1,100.

Rose Window (above entrance): It's Judgment Day, with a tiny Christ in the center of the chaos and miracles that accompany the Apocalyptic last days.

Altar

The altar was raised up high to better display the Crown of Thorns, the relic around which this chapel was built. Notice the staircase: Access was limited to the priest and the king, who wore the keys to the shrine around his neck.

The Crown is supposedly the one placed on Jesus' head as he was being tortured and mocked as "King" of the Jews, before his crucifixion. Legend has it that the Crown was discovered in Jerusalem by Emperor Constantine's mother (circa A.D. 300) and brought to Constantinople (today's Istanbul). There it sat until French Crusaders arrived in the 13th century. King Louis IX, convinced he'd found the real McCoy, paid the equivalent of €500 million for the Crown...and a mere €150 million to build Sainte-Chapelle to house it. Today, the supposed Crown of Thorns is kept by the Notre-Dame Treasury and shown only on Good Friday and on the first Friday of the month at 15:00.

Campaign of Holofernes, one detail of many

Altar for the Crown of Thorns

Before leaving, lay your camera on the ground and shoot the ceiling. Those pure and simple ribs growing out of the slender columns are the essence of Gothic structure.

▶ *Exit Sainte-Chapelle. Back outside, walk counterclockwise around the church to reach the street.*

You'll pass the giant **Palais de Justice,** *now the home of the French Supreme Court. During the Revolution, here is where they enforced the motto* "Liberté, Egalité, Fraternité," *sentencing many to prison in the Conciergerie or to death at the guillotine.*

Now pass through the big iron gate to the noisy Boulevard du Palais. Across the street (and 100 yards farther) is the ⓭ **Cité "Metropolitain"** *Métro stop. This has one of the original early-20th-century subway entrances. It's been preserved as a national art treasure for its curvy, plant-like Art Nouveau ironwork. Nearby is a pleasant flower market.*

Now, from the Palais de Justice, head north a few steps on Boulevard du Palais, and enter the...

⓮ Conciergerie

The Conciergerie was the gloomy prison famous as the last stop for 2,780 victims of the guillotine, including France's last *ancien régime* queen, Marie-Antoinette. Inside, pick up a free map and breeze through.

See the spacious, low-ceilinged Hall of Men-at-Arms (Room 1), used as the guards' dining room. Pass through the bookstore (Room 4 on the map) to find the Office of the Keeper, or "Concierge" of the place (who monitored torture...and recommended nearby restaurants). Next door is the *Toilette,* where condemned prisoners combed their hair or touched up their lipstick before being taken in an open-air cart (tumbrel) to the guillotine on Place de la Concorde.

Upstairs is a memorial room with the names of the 2,780 citizens condemned to death by the guillotine. Find Charlotte Corday ("dite d'Armais"), a noblewoman who snuck into the bathroom of the revolutionary writer Jean-Paul Marat and stabbed him while he bathed. Georges Danton was a prominent revolutionary who was later condemned for being insufficiently liberal—a nasty crime. Louis XVI (called "Capet: last king of France") deserves only a modest mention, as does his wife, Marie-Antoinette. And finally—oh, the irony—there's Maximilien de Robespierre, the head of the Revolution, the man who sent so many to the guillotine before he was eventually toppled, humiliated, imprisoned here, and beheaded.

Back downstairs, you eventually arrive at a re-creation of Marie-Antoinette's cell. Mannequins, period furniture, and a video set the scene. Imagine the queen spending her last days—separated from her 10-year-old son, and now widowed because the king had already been executed. The guard stands modestly behind a screen, while the queen psyches herself up with a crucifix. On October 16, 1793, the queen stepped onto the cart, and was slowly carried to Place de la Concorde, where she had a date with "Monsieur de Paris"—the guillotine.

▶ *Back outside, turn left on Boulevard du Palais and head north. On the corner is the city's oldest public clock, from 1334.*

Turn left onto Quai de l'Horloge and walk west along the river. The bridge up ahead is the Pont Neuf, where we'll end this walk. At the first corner, veer left into a sleepy triangular square called…

Original Art Nouveau Métro entrance

Marie-Antoinette's cell in the Conciergerie

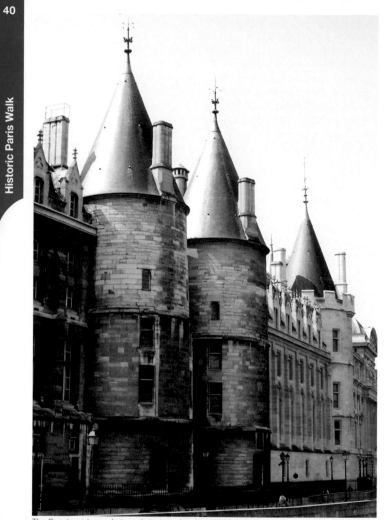

The Conciergerie—a photogenic torture chamber—held prisoners awaiting the guillotine.

⓯ Place Dauphine

It's amazing to find such coziness in the heart of Paris. This city of two million is still a city of neighborhoods, a collection of villages. The French Supreme Court building looms behind like a giant marble gavel. The Caveau du Palais restaurant is a nice spot for a drink or light meal. You may see lawyers on their lunch break lobbing metal balls at a target, playing *boules*.

▶ *Continue through Place Dauphine. As you pop out the other end, you're face-to-face with a* **statue of Henry IV** *(1553-1610). Though not as famous as his grandson, Louis XIV, Henry helped make Paris what it is today—a European capital of elegant buildings (such as the Louvre's Grand Gallery), quiet squares (such as Place Dauphine), and majestic bridges...such as the Pont Neuf, to your right. Walk onto the bridge and pause at the little nook halfway across.*

⓰ Pont Neuf and the Seine

This "new bridge" is now Paris' oldest. Built during Henry IV's reign (about 1600), its arches span the widest part of the river. Unlike other bridges, this one never had houses or buildings growing on it. The turrets were originally for vendors and street entertainers. From the bridge, look downstream (west) to see the next bridge, the pedestrian-only Pont des Arts, a popular gathering spot in the evening (as is the prow-shaped tip of the Ile de la Cité to your left—one of Paris' favorite make-out spots). Ahead on the Right Bank is the long Louvre Museum. Beyond that, on the Left Bank, is the Orsay. And what's that tall black tower in the distance?

Our walk ends where Paris began—on the Seine River. Stretching from Dijon to the English Channel, the Seine meanders 500 miles, cutting through the center of Paris. The river is shallow and slow within the city, but still dangerous enough to require steep stone embankments (built in 1910) to prevent occasional floods.

The banks of the Seine are becoming increasingly pedestrian-friendly. On the Left Bank is a pleasant stretch from the Orsay to Pont de l'Alma. On the Right Bank, the Hôtel de Ville area is nice. In summer, certain paved areas are covered with acres of sand, beach chairs, and tanned locals, creating the *Paris Plages* (Paris Beaches). Any time of year, you'll see tourist boats and the commercial barges that carry 20 percent of Paris' transported goods. And on the banks, sportsmen today cast into the waters once fished by Paris' original Celtic inhabitants.

▶ *We're done. From here, you could take a boat tour (Vedettes du Pont Neuf) leaving from near the base of Pont Neuf on the island side. The Pont Neuf Métro stop is across the bridge on the Right Bank. Bus #69 heads east along Quai du Louvre (at the north end of the bridge) and west along Rue de Rivoli (a block farther north). In fact, you can go anywhere—you're standing in the heart of Paris.*

Pont Neuf—400-year old "new bridge"

Louvre Tour

Musée du Louvre

Paris' world-class museums walk you through world history, and the best place to start your "art-yssey" is at the Louvre. With more than 30,000 works of art, the Louvre is a full inventory of Western civilization. To cover it all in one visit is impossible. Let's focus on the Louvre's specialties—Greek sculpture, Italian painting, and French painting.

We'll see "Venuses" through history, from prehistoric stick figures to the curvy *Venus de Milo* to the wind-blown *Winged Victory of Samothrace,* from placid medieval Madonnas to the *Mona Lisa* to the symbol of modern democracy. Each generation defined beauty differently, and we'll gain insight into long-ago civilizations by admiring what they found beautiful.

ORIENTATION

Cost: €12, free on first Sun of month, covered by Museum Pass. Tickets good all day; re-entry allowed.

Hours: Wed-Mon 9:00-18:00, Wed and Fri until 21:45, closed Tue, last entry 45 minutes before closing. Galleries begin closing 30 minutes before official closing time.

When to Go: Crowds are worst on Sun, Mon, Wed, and mornings. In the evenings, crowds are manageable.

Getting There: Métro stop Palais Royal-Musée du Louvre is the closest. Handy bus #69 heading east from Rue Cler to the Marais stops along the Seine River at Quai François Mitterand. Westbound bus #69 stops along Rue de Rivoli at the Palais Royal-Musée du Louvre Métro stop (where you'll also find a taxi stand).

Getting In:

Main Pyramid Entrance: There is no grander entry than through the glass pyramid in the central courtyard, but long lines can form at security.

Museum Pass/Group Entrance: Museum Pass holders can use the group entrance in the pedestrian passageway (labeled *Pavilion Richelieu*) between the pyramid and Rue de Rivoli. It's under the arches, a few steps north of the pyramid; find the uniformed guard at the security checkpoint entrance, at the down escalator.

Underground Mall Entrance: Anyone can use the less crowded underground entrance located within the Carrousel du Louvre shopping mall at 99 Rue de Rivoli (the door with the red awning). You can also reach the mall directly from the Métro stop Palais Royal-Musée du

Main Pyramid Entrance

The underground mall entrance is less crowded.

Louvre Overview

200 Meters
200 Yards

PALAIS ROYAL

Place du Palais Royal

RUE ST. HONORE

RICHELIEU WING

Palais Royal-Musée du Louvre

PEDESTRIAN PASSAGEWAY

#69

Louvre-Rivoli

Tuileries Garden

ARC DU CARROUSEL

NEAR EASTERN

FRENCH

Cour Carrée

RUE DE L'AMIRAL DE COLIGNY

AXIS VIEW

MAIN ENTRANCE

PYRAMID

LOUIS XIV

FORMER TUILERIES PALACE

ITALIAN & FRENCH

GREEK

WINGED VICTORY

CAFES

DENON WING

QUAI FRANÇOIS MITTERRAND

#69

Seine River

QUAI VOLTAIRE

← To Orsay Museum (15 min. walk)

LEFT

QUAI MALAQUAIS

BANK

To Latin Quarter (10 min. walk)

→ One-Way Street

1 Main Pyramid Entrance
2 Museum Pass/Group Entrace
3 Underground Mall Entrance
4 Café le Nemours
5 Le Fumoir

Louvre Tour

Louvre: Stepping off the train, exit following signs to *Musée du Louvre-Le Carrousel du Louvre.* At the Louvre entrance, Museum Pass-holders can skip to the head of the security line.

Buying Tickets: Self-serve ticket machines located under the pyramid are faster to use than the ticket windows (machines accept euro notes, coins, and chip-and-PIN Visa cards). The *tabac* in the underground mall sells tickets and Museum Passes (cash only).

Information: Tel. 01 40 20 53 17, recorded info tel. 01 40 20 51 51, louvre.fr.

Tours: Ninety-minute guided tours leave daily (except the first Sun of the month) at 11:00 and 14:00 from the **Accueil des Groupes** area under the pyramid (€9 plus your entry ticket, tel. 01 40 20 52 63). Videoguides are €5. Or you can download a free Rick Steves **audio tour** (✪ see page 207).

Length of This Tour: Allow at least two hours.

Baggage Check: Large bags must be checked (it's free), and you can also check small bags to lighten your load. You can't check cameras, money, passports, or other valuables.

Services: WCs are located under the pyramid. Once you're in the galleries, WCs are scarce.

Photography: Photography without a flash is allowed.

Cuisine Art: The Louvre has several cafés. The best is **Café Mollien,** located near the end of our tour (€12 for sandwich and drink on terrace overlooking pyramid). A self-service lunch **cafeteria** (reasonable *plats du jour*) is up the escalator from the pyramid in the Richelieu wing. The **Carrousel du Louvre** underground shopping mall (west of the pyramid) has a food-court upstairs with decent-value, multiethnic fast-food eateries. Outside the Louvre, try the venerable **Café le Nemours** or the classy **Le Fumoir,** or **picnic** in the Palais Royal courtyards (✪ see page 186).

Quick Tips: Expect changes to this tour, as the Louvre's massive collection is constantly in flux—paintings in restoration, rooms closed, a renovation of the pyramid entrance, etc. Concentrate on the biggies, and try to finish the tour with enough energy left to browse.

Starring: *Venus de Milo, Winged Victory, Mona Lisa,* Leonardo da Vinci, Raphael, Michelangelo, the French painters, and many of the most iconic images of Western civilization.

THE TOUR BEGINS

▶ *Start under the glass pyramid—pick up a free map at the information desk and get oriented.*

The Louvre, the largest museum in the Western world, fills three wings of this immense, U-shaped palace. The **Richelieu wing** (north side) houses Oriental Antiquities, plus French, Dutch, and Northern art. The **Sully wing** (east side) has extensive French painting and ancient Egypt collections.

We'll concentrate on the Louvre's south side: the **Denon** and **Sully** wings, which hold many of the superstars, including ancient Greek sculpture, Italian Renaissance painting, and French Neoclassical and Romantic painting.

▶ *From the pyramid, head for the Denon wing. Ride the escalator up one floor. After showing your ticket, take the first left, follow the Antiquités Grecques signs, and climb a set of stairs to the brick-ceilinged Salle (Room) 1: Grèce Préclassique. Enter prehistory.*

GREECE (3000 B.C.-A.D. 1)

Pre-Classical Greek Statues

These statues are noble but crude. In the first glass cases, find Greek Barbie dolls (3000 B.C.) that are older than the pyramids. These pre-rational voodoo dolls whittle women down to their life-giving traits. Halfway down the hall, a woman *(Dame d'Auxerre)* pledges allegiance to stability. Farther along, another woman *(Kore)* is essentially a column with breasts. The

The Louvre—Pre-Classical Greece

PYRAMID

START

N

Not to Scale

TICKET
TAKER

DENON
WING

PRE-CLASSICAL GREECE
SALLE 1-3

To
Golden Age
Greece

GREEK
BARBIE
DOLLS

DAME
D'AUXERRE

KORE

*Alternate Route
To Greek Statues*

To Arts de l'Islam

early Greeks, who admired statues like these, found stability more attractive than movement. A young, naked man *(Kouros)* is so stiff he seems to have a gun to his back—"Don't move."

But around 500 B.C., Greece entered its Golden Age, a cultural explosion that changed the course of history. Over the next 500 years, Greece produced art that was rational, orderly, and balanced. The balance between timeless stability and fleeting movement made beauty. Most of the art that we'll see in the Louvre either came from Greece or was inspired by it.

▶ *Let's head for one of the ancient world's finest statues. Exit at the far end of the pre-Classical Greece galleries, and climb the stairs one flight. At the top, veer left (toward 11 o'clock), and continue into the Sully wing. After about 50 yards, turn right into Salle 16, where you'll find Venus de Milo floating above a sea of worshipping tourists. It's been said that among the warlike Greeks, this was the first statue to unilaterally disarm.*

Venus de Milo (*Aphrodite,* late 2nd century B.C.)

The *Venus de Milo* (or goddess of love, from the Greek island of Melos) created a sensation when it was discovered in 1820. Europe was already in the grip of a classical fad, and this statue seemed to sum up all that ancient Greece stood for. The optimistic Greeks pictured their gods in human form (meaning humans are godlike), and Venus' well-proportioned body captures the perfection of the Greek universe.

Split *Venus* down the middle from nose to toes and see how the two halves balance each other. Venus rests on her right foot (called *contrapposto,* or "counterpoise"), then lifts her left leg, setting her whole body in motion. As the left leg rises, her right shoulder droops down. And as her knee points one way, her head turns the other, giving a pleasing S-curve

Venus de Milo—balance of opposites

Athena in the Gallery of Statues

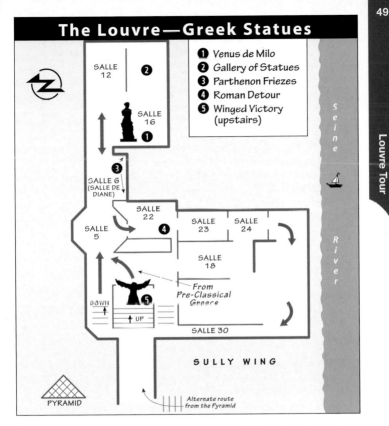

The Louvre—Greek Statues

1. Venus de Milo
2. Gallery of Statues
3. Parthenon Friezes
4. Roman Detour
5. Winged Victory (upstairs)

SALLE 12

SALLE 16

SALLE 6 (SALLE DE DIANE)

SALLE 22

SALLE 5

SALLE 23

SALLE 24

SALLE 18

From Pre-Classical Greece

DOWN

UP

SALLE 30

SULLY WING

PYRAMID

Alternate route from the Pyramid

Seine River

to her body (especially noticeable from the back). *Venus* is a harmonious balance of opposites, orbiting slowly around a vertical axis.

Other opposites balance as well, like the smooth skin of her upper half that sets off the rough-cut texture of her dress (size 14). She's actually made from two different pieces of stone plugged together at the hips (the seam is visible). The face is anatomically accurate, but it's also idealized, a perfect goddess. This isn't any particular woman, but Everywoman—all the idealized features that appealed to the Greeks.

What were her missing arms doing? Some say her right arm held her dress, while her left arm was raised. Others say she was hugging a male statue or leaning on a column. I say she was picking her navel.

▶ *Orbit* Venus. *This statue is interesting and different from every angle. Remember the view from the back—we'll see it again later. Now make your reentry to earth. Follow Venus' gaze and browse around the adjoining rooms (15, 14, and 13) of this long hall.*

Gallery of Statues

You'll see statues of gods, satyrs, soldiers, athletes, and everyday people engaged in ordinary activities. Greek statues feature the human body in all its splendor. The anatomy is accurate, and the poses are relaxed and natural. Greek sculptors learned to capture people in motion, and to show them from different angles, not just face-forward. The classic *contrapposto* pose—with the weight resting on one leg—captures a balance between timeless stability and fleeting motion.

For Athenians, the most popular goddess was their patron, Athena. She's usually shown as a warrior, wearing a helmet and carrying a spear, ready to fight for her city. Whatever the statue, Golden Age artists sought the perfect balance between down-to-earth humans (with human flaws and quirks) and the idealized perfection of a Greek god.

▶ *Head for Salle 6 (also known as Salle de Diane), located behind the* Venus de Milo. *(Facing* Venus, *make a loop to the right, of about 20 paces.) You'll find two carved panels on the wall.*

Parthenon Frieze (*Les Sculptures du Parthenon,* c. 440 B.C.)

These stone fragments once decorated the exterior of the greatest Athenian temple, the Parthenon, built at the peak of the Greek Golden Age. A model of the Parthenon shows where the panels might have hung. The centaur panel would have gone above the entrance. The panel of girls was placed under the covered colonnade, but above the doorway (you'll have to crouch way down and look up to see the frieze of panels).

One panel shows a centaur sexually harassing a woman, telling the story of how these rude creatures crashed a party of humans. But the Greeks fought back and threw the brutes out, just as Athens (metaphorically) conquered its barbarian neighbors and became civilized.

The other relief shows the sacred procession of young girls who marched up the hill every four years with an embroidered veil for the

Parthenon frieze—natural movement

Roman busts—warts-and-all realism

40-foot-high statue of Athena, the goddess of wisdom. Carved in only a couple of inches of stone, they're amazingly realistic. They glide along horizontally (their belts and shoulders all in a line), while the folds of their dresses drape down vertically, like fluted columns. The man in the center is relaxed, realistic, and *contrapposto*. Notice the veins in his arm. These carved figures pose and move naturally, their human forms emerging gracefully from the stone.

▸ *Make another 20-step loop into the nearby Salle 5 and turn left into Salle 22, the Roman Antiquities room (Antiquités Romaines), for a...*

Roman Detour (Salles 22-30)

Stroll among the Caesars and try to see the person behind the public persona. Besides the many faces of the ubiquitous Emperor *Inconnu* ("unknown"), you might spot Augustus (Auguste), the first emperor, and his wily wife, Livia (Livie). Their son Tiberius (Tibère) was the Caesar that Jesus Christ "rendered unto." Caligula was notoriously depraved, curly-haired Domitia murdered her husband, Hadrian popularized the beard, Trajan ruled the Empire at its peak, and Marcus Aurelius (Marc Aurèle) presided stoically over Rome's slow fall.

The pragmatic Romans (500 B.C.-A.D. 500) were great conquerors but bad artists. One area in which they excelled was realistic portrait busts, especially of their emperors, who were worshipped as gods on earth. The Romans also loved Greek statues and made countless copies, adding a veneer of sophistication to their homes, temples, and offices.

▸ *To reach the* Winged Victory, *get out your map, or just continue clockwise through the Roman collection of sarcophagi and mosaics, which eventually spills out at the base of the stairs leading up to the first floor and the dramatic...*

Winged Victory of Samothrace (*Victoire de Samothrace,* c. 190 B.C.)

This woman with wings, poised on the prow of a ship, once stood on a hilltop to commemorate a naval victory. Her clothes are windblown and sea-sprayed, clinging close enough to her body to win a wet T-shirt contest. Originally, her right arm was stretched high, celebrating the victory like a Super Bowl champion, waving a "we're number one" finger.

This is the *Venus de Milo* gone Hellenistic, from the time after the culture of Athens was spread around the Mediterranean by Alexander the Great (c. 325 B.C.). As *Victory* strides forward, the wind blows her and her wings back. Her feet are firmly on the ground, but her wings (and missing arms) stretch upward. She is a pillar of vertical strength, while the clothes curve and whip around her. These opposing forces create a feeling of great energy, making her the lightest two-ton piece of rock in captivity.

In the glass case nearby is *Victory*'s open right hand with an outstretched finger, found in Turkey in 1950, a century after the statue itself was unearthed. The French negotiated with the Turkish government for the rights to it. Considering all the other ancient treasures that France had looted from Turkey in the past, the Turks thought it only appropriate to give the French the finger.

▶ *Enter the octagonal room to the left as you face the* Winged Victory, *with Icarus bungee-jumping from the ceiling. Find a friendly window and look out toward the pyramid.*

Winged Victory—wind-blown exuberance

Crown jewels in the Apollo Gallery

View from the Octagonal Room: The Louvre as a Palace

The former royal palace, the Louvre was built in stages over eight centuries. On your right (the eastern Sully wing) was the original medieval fortress. About 500 yards to the west, in the now-open area past the pyramid and the triumphal arch, is where the Tuileries Palace used to stand. Succeeding kings tried to connect these two palaces, each one adding another section onto the long, skinny north and south wings. Finally, in 1852, after three centuries of building, the two palaces were connected, creating a rectangular Louvre. Nineteen years later, the Tuileries Palace burned down during a riot, leaving the U-shaped Louvre we see today. During the Revolution, the citizens beheaded the king, inherited his palace and art collection, opened the doors to the masses, and *voilà!* You have Europe's first public museum.

The glass pyramid was designed by the Chinese-born American architect I. M. Pei (1989). Many Parisians hated the pyramid, just as they hated another new and controversial structure 100 years ago—the Eiffel Tower.

▶ *From the octagonal room, enter the Apollo Gallery (Galerie d'Apollon).*

Apollo Gallery

This gallery gives us a feel for the Louvre as the glorious home of French kings (before Versailles). Imagine a chandelier-lit party in this room, drenched in stucco and gold leaf, with tapestries of leading Frenchmen and paintings featuring mythological and symbolic themes. The crystal vases, the inlaid tables, and many other art objects, show the wealth of France, Europe's number-one power for two centuries.

Stroll past glass cases of royal dinnerware to the far end of the room. In a glass case are France's crown jewels. The display varies, but you may see the jewel-studded crown of Louis XV (a.k.a. "The Crown of Charlemagne") and the 140-carat Regent Diamond, which once graced crowns worn by Louis XV, Louis XVI, and Napoleon.

▶ *A rare WC is several rooms away, near Salle 38 in the Sully wing. The Italian collection (Peintures Italiennes) is on the other side of Winged Victory. Cross back in front of Winged Victory to Salle 1, where you'll find two **Botticelli frescoes** that give us a preview of how ancient Greece would be "reborn" in the Renaissance. Now continue into the large Salle 3.*

THE MEDIEVAL WORLD (1200-1500)

Cimabue—*The Madonna of the Angels* (1280)

During the Age of Faith (1200s), almost every church in Europe had a painting like this one. Mary was a cult figure—even bigger than the 20th-century Madonna—adored and prayed to by the faithful for bringing baby Jesus into the world. The medieval world—still suffering from the collapse of the Roman Empire (c. A.D. 500)—was a poor and violent place, with the Christian Church as the only constant in troubled times.

Altarpieces tended to follow the same formula: somber iconic faces, stiff poses, elegant folds in the robes, and generic angels. Cimabue's holy figures are laid flat on a gold background like cardboard cutouts, existing in a golden never-never land, as though the faithful couldn't imagine them as flesh-and-blood humans inhabiting our dark and sinful earth.

Giotto—*St. Francis of Assisi Receiving the Stigmata* (c. 1290-1295)

Francis of Assisi (c. 1181-1226), a wandering Italian monk of renowned goodness, kneels on a rocky Italian hillside, pondering the pain of Christ's torture and execution. Suddenly, he looks up, startled, to see Christ himself, with six wings, hovering above. Christ shoots lasers from his wounds to the hands, feet, and side of the empathetic monk, marking him with the stigmata. Francis went on to breathe the spirit of the Renaissance into medieval Europe. His humble love of man and nature inspired artists like Giotto to portray real human beings with real emotions, living in a physical world of beauty.

Like a good filmmaker, Giotto (c. 1266-1337, JOT-toh) doesn't just *tell*

Cimabue—2-D cardboard cutouts

Giotto—hints of 3-D and humanism

us what happened, he *shows* us in the present tense, freezing the scene at its most dramatic moment. Though the perspective is crude—Francis' hut is smaller than he is, and Christ is somehow shooting at Francis while facing us—Giotto creates the illusion of 3-D, with a foreground (Francis), middle ground (his hut), and background (the hillside). In the predella (the panel of paintings below the altarpiece), Francis gives a sermon in the open-air, while birds gather at his feet to catch a few words from the beloved hippie of Assisi.

▶ *The long Grand Gallery displays Italian Renaissance painting—some masterpieces, some not.*

ITALIAN RENAISSANCE

The Grand Gallery
Built in the late 1500s to connect the old palace with the Tuileries Palace, the Grand Gallery displays much of the Louvre's Italian Renaissance art. From the doorway, look to the far end and consider this challenge: I hold the world's record for the Grand Gallery Heel-Toe-Fun-Walk-Tourist-Slalom, going end-to-end in 1 minute, 58 seconds (only two injured). Time yourself. Along the way, notice some of the general features of Italian Renaissance painting:

- **Religious:** You'll see lots of Madonnas, martyrs, and saints.

- **Symmetrical:** The Madonnas are flanked by saints—two to the left, two to the right, and so on.

- **Realistic:** Real-life human features are especially obvious in the occasional portrait.

- **Three-Dimensional:** Every scene gets a spacious setting with a distant horizon.

- **Classical:** You'll see some Greek gods and classical nudes, but even Christian saints pose like Greek statues, and Mary is a *Venus* whose face and gestures embody all that was good in the Christian world.

Andrea Mantegna—*St. Sebastian* (c. 1480)
This isn't the patron saint of acupuncture. St. Sebastian was a Christian martyr, killed by the pagan Romans for his beliefs. Though Christian, here he looks more like a classical Greek statue. Notice the *contrapposto* stance

The Louvre—Grand Gallery

DENON WING

WC

Stairs Down to ⓭

Ⓒ A F E

GRAND GALLERY

Courtyard

Ⓒ

FRENCH ROMANTICISM
(SALLE MOLLIEN)

⓫

DIANA STATUE

SALLE DES ETATS

SALLE DENON

Ⓒ

ITALIAN RENAISSANCE

⑧ ⑦

PYRAMID

Courtyard

⑩

FRENCH NEOCLASSICISM
(SALLE DARU)

⑤

⑨

Stairs Down to Greek Statues & Roman Collection

④

30 Meters

30 Yards

SALON CARREE

ROMAN MOSAIC (BELOW)

③

②

①

APOLLO GALLERY

OCTAGONAL ROOM

Seine River

① BOTTICELLI – Frescoes
② CIMABUE – The Madonna and Child in Majesty
③ GIOTTO – St. Francis of Assisi
④ MANTEGNA – St. Sebastian
⑤ LEONARDO – The Virgin and Child with St. Anne

⑥ RAPHAEL – La Belle Jardinière
⑦ LEONARDO – Mona Lisa
⑧ VERONESE – The Marriage at Cana
⑨ DAVID – The Coronation of Emperor Napoleon
⑩ INGRES – La Grande Odalisque
⑪ GERICAULT – The Raft of the Medusa
⑫ DELACROIX – Liberty Leading the People
⑬ MICHELANGELO – Slaves

A victim of persecution

A victim of the Louvre

(all of his weight resting on one leg) and the Greek ruins scattered around him. His executioners look like ignorant medieval brutes bewildered by this enlightened man. Let the Renaissance begin.

▶ Look for the following masterpieces by Leonardo 50 yards down the Grand Gallery, on the left.

Leonardo da Vinci—The *Virgin and Child with St. Anne* (*La Vierge à l'Enfant Jésus avec Sainte-Anne*, c. 1510)

Three generations—grandmother, mother, and child—are arranged in a pyramid, with Anne's face as the peak and the lamb as the lower-right corner. Within this balanced structure, Leonardo sets the figures in motion: Anne's legs point one way, her daughter Mary reaches the opposite way, Jesus playfully turns toward Mary, while the lamb pulls away from him. But even with all the twisting and turning, this is still a placid scene. It's as orderly as the geometrically perfect universe created by the Renaissance god.

There's a psychological kidney punch in this happy painting. Jesus, the picture of childish joy, is innocently playing with a lamb—the symbol of his inevitable sacrificial death.

The Louvre has the greatest collection of Leonardos in the world—five of them. Look for the neighboring *Virgin of the Rocks* and *John the Baptist.* Leonardo spent his final years in France as the beloved court painter for King Francois I. Leonardo was the consummate Renaissance man: a musician, sculptor, engineer, scientist, and sometime painter, he combined knowledge from all of these areas to create beauty. If he were alive today, he'd create a Unified Field Theory in physics—and set it to music.

Leonardo's *The Virgin and Child with St. Anne*—three generations of love

▶ *You'll likely find Raphael's art on the right side of the Grand Gallery, just past the statue of* Diana the Huntress.

Raphael—*La Belle Jardinière* (1507)

Raphael (roff-eye-ELL) perfected the style Leonardo pioneered. The Madonna, Child, and John the Baptist form a Leonard-esque pyramid, and the scene is softened with a hazy grace. Mary is a mountain of maternal tenderness (the title translates as "The Beautiful Gardener"), as she eyes her son with a knowing look and holds his hand in a gesture of union. Jesus looks up innocently, standing *contrapposto* like a chubby Greek statue. Baby John the Baptist kneels lovingly at Jesus' feet, holding a cross that hints at his playmate's sacrificial death. The interplay of gestures and gazes gives the masterpiece both intimacy and cohesiveness, while Raphael's blended brushstrokes varnish the work with an iridescent smoothness.

Raphael adopted Leonardo's trademark pyramid composition for *La Belle Jardinière*.

Italian Renaissance (1400-1600)

A thousand years after Rome fell, plunging Europe into the Dark Ages, the Greek ideal of beauty was reborn in 15th-century Italy. The Renaissance—or "rebirth" of the culture of ancient Greece and Rome—was a cultural boom that changed people's thinking about every aspect of life. In politics, it meant democracy. In religion, it meant a move away from Church dominance and toward the assertion of man (humanism) and a more personal faith. Science and secular learning were revived after centuries of superstition and ignorance. In architecture, it was a return to the balanced columns and domes of Greece and Rome.

In painting, the Renaissance meant realism, and for the Italians, realism was spelled "3-D." Artists rediscovered the beauty of nature and the human body. With pictures of beautiful people in harmonious 3-D surroundings, they expressed the optimism and confidence of this new age.

With Raphael, the Greek ideal of beauty—reborn in the Renaissance—reached its peak. His work spawned so many imitators who cranked out sickly sweet, generic Madonnas that we often take him for granted. Don't. This is the real thing.

▶ *The* Mona Lisa (La Joconde) *is near the statue of* Diana, *in Salle 6—the Salle des Etats—midway down the Grand Gallery on the right. Mona sits alone behind glass, as six million heavy-breathing people crowd in each year to ogle her. (You can't miss her. Just follow the signs and the people...it's the only painting you can hear. With all the groveling crowds, you can even smell it.)*

Leonardo da Vinci—*Mona Lisa* (1503-1506)

When François I invited Leonardo to France, the artist—determined to pack light—brought only a few of his paintings. One was a portrait of Lisa del Giocondo, the 20-something wife of a wealthy Florentine businessman. François immediately fell in love with the painting, making it the centerpiece of the small collection of Italian masterpieces that would, in three centuries, become the Louvre museum. He called it *La Gioconda* (*La Joconde* in French)—both her last name and a play on the Italian word for "happy woman." We know it as a contraction of the Italian for "my lady Lisa"—*Mona Lisa.*

Mona may disappoint you. She's smaller than you'd expect, darker, engulfed in a huge room, and hidden behind a glaring pane of glass. So why all the hubbub? Let's take a closer look. As you would with any lover, you've got to accept her for what she is, not what you'd like her to be.

The famous smile attracts you first. Leonardo used a hazy technique called *sfumato,* blurring the edges of her mysterious smile. Try as you might, you can never quite see the corners of her mouth. Is she happy? Sad? Tender? Or is it a cynical supermodel's smirk? All visitors read it differently, projecting their own moods onto her enigmatic face. *Mona* is a Rorschach inkblot...so, how are you feeling?

Now look past the smile and the eyes that really do follow you (most eyes in portraits do) to some of the subtle Renaissance elements that make this painting work. The body is surprisingly massive and statue-like, a perfectly balanced pyramid turned at an angle, so we can see its mass. Her arm is resting lightly on the chair's armrest, almost on the level of the frame itself, as if she's sitting in a window looking out at us. The folds of her sleeves and her gently folded hands are remarkably realistic and relaxed. The typical Leonardo landscape shows distance by getting hazier and hazier.

Though the portrait is most likely of Lisa del Giocondo, there are many other hypotheses about her identity, including the idea that it's Leonardo himself. Or she might be the Mama Lisa. A recent infrared scan revealed that she has a barely visible veil over her dress, which may mean (in the custom of the day) that she had just had a baby.

The overall mood is one of balance and serenity, but there's also an

Leonardo's *Mona Lisa*

Veronese's Venetian party scene

element of mystery. *Mona*'s smile and long-distance beauty are subtle and elusive, tempting but always just out of reach, like strands of a street singer's melody drifting through the Métro tunnel. *Mona* doesn't knock your socks off, but she winks at the patient viewer.

▶ *Before leaving* Mona, *step back and just observe the paparazzi scene. The huge canvas opposite* Mona *is...*

Paolo Veronese—*The Marriage at Cana* (1562-1563)

Stand 10 steps away from this enormous canvas to where it just fills your field of vision, and suddenly...you're in a party! Help yourself to a glass of wine. This is the Renaissance love of beautiful things gone hog-wild.

In a spacious setting of Renaissance architecture, colorful lords and ladies, decked out in their fanciest duds, feast on a great spread of food and drink, while the musicians fuel the fires of good fun. Servants prepare and serve the food, jesters play, and animals roam. In the upper left, a dog and his master look on. A sturdy linebacker in yellow pours wine out of a jug (right foreground). The man in white samples some wine and thinks, "Hmm, not bad," while nearby a ferocious cat battles a lion. The wedding couple at the far left is almost forgotten.

Believe it or not, this is a religious work showing the wedding celebration in which Jesus turned water into wine. And there's Jesus in the dead center of 130 frolicking figures, wondering if maybe beer might have been a better choice. With true Renaissance optimism, Venetians pictured Christ as a party animal, someone who loved the created world as much as they did.

Now, let's hear it for the band! On bass—the bad cat with the funny hat—Titian the Venetian! And joining him on viola—Crazy Veronese!

▶ *Exit behind* Mona *into the Salle Denon (Room 76). The dramatic Romantic room is to your left, and the grand Neoclassical room is to your right. Entering the Neoclassical room (Salle Daru), kneel before the largest canvas in the Louvre.*

FRENCH NEOCLASSICISM (1780-1850)

Jacques-Louis David—*The Coronation of Napoleon* (1806-1807)

Napoleon holds aloft an imperial crown. This common-born son of immigrants is about to be crowned emperor of a "New Rome." He has just made his wife, Josephine, the empress, and she kneels at his feet. Seated behind Napoleon is the pope, who journeyed from Rome to place the imperial crown on his head. But Napoleon feels that no one is worthy of the task. At the last moment, he shrugs the pope aside, grabs the crown, holds it up for all to see...and crowns himself. The pope looks p.o.'d.

After the French people decapitated their king during the Revolution (1793), their fledgling democracy floundered in chaos. France was united by a charismatic, brilliant, temperamental, upstart general who kept his feet on the ground, his eyes on the horizon, and his hand in his coat—Napoleon

Napoleon (center) crowns himself and his wife Josephine (kneeling) while the pope looks on.

Bonaparte. Napoleon quickly conquered most of Europe and insisted on being made emperor.

The painter David (dah-VEED) recorded the coronation for posterity. (Find his self-portrait using the key on the picture frame telling who's who. He's way up in the second balcony, peeking around the tassel directly above Napoleon's crown.) David was the new emperor's official painter and propagandist, in charge of color-coordinating the costumes and flags for public spectacles. The coronation ceremony took place in Notre-Dame cathedral, which was fitted with fake columns and arches to reflect the glories of Greece and the grandeur of Rome. As a painter, David's simple style and Greek themes championed the "Neoclassical" style that influenced generations of artists.

The radiant woman in the gallery in the background center is Napoleon's mom. Since she couldn't make it to Paris to watch her boy become the most powerful man in Europe, Napoleon had David paint his mom in later.

▶ *As you double back toward the Romantic room, pause at Jean-Auguste-Dominique Ingres'* **La Grande Odalisque (1819)**—*a horizontal take on* **Venus de Milo**'s *backside. Continue on, crossing back through the Salle Denon and into Room 77, gushing with...*

FRENCH ROMANTICISM (1800-1850)

Théodore Géricault—*The Raft of the Medusa* (*Le Radeau de la Méduse,* 1819)

In the artistic war between hearts and minds, the heart style was known as Romanticism. Stressing motion and emotion, it was the flip side of cool, balanced Neoclassicism, though they both flourished in the early 1800s.

What better setting for an emotional work than a shipwreck? Clinging to a raft is a tangle of bodies sprawled over each other. The scene writhes with agitated, ominous motion—the ripple of muscles, churning clouds, and choppy seas. On the right, a deathly green corpse dangles overboard. The face of the man at left, cradling a dead body, says it all—the despair of spending weeks stranded in the middle of nowhere.

This painting was based on an actual event—150 shipwrecked people were set adrift on the open seas for 12 days, suffering hardship and hunger, even resorting to cannibalism. The story was made to order for a

Ingres' *Odalisque*—cool Neoclassicism

Géricault's *Raft*—fevered Romanticism

painter determined to shock the public—young Géricault (ZHAIR-ee-ko). To reproduce the raw emotion, he interviewed survivors. He sketched dead bodies in the morgue and the twisted faces of lunatics in asylums, capturing the moment when all hope is lost.

But wait. There's a stir in the crowd. They've spotted something. The bodies rise up in a pyramid of hope, culminating in a waving flag. They signal frantically, trying to catch the attention of the tiny ship on the horizon, their last desperate hope...which did finally save them. If art controls your heartbeat, this is a masterpiece.

Eugène Delacroix—*Liberty Leading the People* (*La Liberté Guidant le Peuple,* 1830)

The year is 1830. King Charles has been restored to the throne after Napoleon's exile, and his subjects are angry. The Parisians take to the streets once again, *Les Miz*–style, to fight royalist oppressors. Leading them on through the smoke and over the dead and dying is the figure of Liberty, a strong woman waving the French flag. Does this symbol of victory look familiar? It's the *Winged Victory,* wingless and topless. Delacroix shows the full range of France's social classes—the hard-bitten proletarian with a sword (far left), an intellectual with a top hat and a sawed-off shotgun, and even a little boy brandishing pistols. Eventually, the people would triumph, replacing the king with Louis-Philippe, who was happy to rule within the constraints of a modern constitution.

To stir our emotions, Delacroix (del-ah-kwah) uses only three major colors—the red, white, and blue of the French flag. France is the symbol of Revolution and modern democracy, and this painting has long stirred its citizens' passion for liberty.

Delacroix's *Lady Liberty*—in the classic pose of the Winged Victory—leads the French onward.

This symbol of freedom is a fitting tribute to the Louvre, the first museum ever opened to the common rabble of humanity. The good things in life don't belong only to a small, wealthy part of society, but to everyone. The motto of France is *Liberté, Egalité, Fraternité*—liberty, equality, and brotherhood for all.

▶ *Exit the room at the far end (past the Café Mollien) and go downstairs, where you'll bump into the bum of a large, twisting male nude looking like he's just waking up after a thousand-year nap.*

EPILOGUE

Michelangelo—*Slaves* (1513-1515)
These two statues by earth's greatest sculptor are an appropriate end to this museum—works that bridge the ancient and modern worlds.

Michelangelo, like his fellow Renaissance artists, learned from the Greeks. The perfect anatomy, twisting poses, and idealized faces appear as if they could have been created 2,000 years earlier.

The so-called *Dying Slave* (also called the *Sleeping Slave*, looking like he should be stretched out on a sofa) twists listlessly against his T-shirt-like bonds, revealing his smooth skin. Compare the polished detail of the rippling, bulging left arm with the sketchy details of the face and neck. With Michelangelo, the body does the talking. This is probably the most sensual nude Michelangelo, the master of the male body, ever created.

The *Rebellious Slave* fights against his bondage. His shoulders rotate one way, his head and leg turn the other. He looks upward, straining to get free. He even seems to be trying to free himself from the rock he's made of. Michelangelo said that his purpose was to carve away the marble to reveal the figures God put inside. This slave shows the agony of that process and the ecstasy of the result.

▶ *Tour over! These two may be slaves of the museum, but you are free to go or browse at your leisure. To leave the museum, head for the end of the hall, turn right, and follow signs down the escalators to the Sortie.*

Michelangelo's *Slaves* bridges the ancient and modern worlds.

Orsay Museum Tour

Musée d'Orsay

The Musée d'Orsay (mew-zay dor-say), housing French art from 1848-1914, picks up where the Louvre's art collection leaves off. That means Impressionism, the art of sun-dappled fields, bright colors, and crowded Parisian cafés. The Orsay houses the best general collection anywhere of Manet, Monet, Renoir, Degas, Van Gogh, Cézanne, and Gauguin. If you like Impressionism, visit this museum. If you don't like Impressionism, visit this museum. I personally find it a more enjoyable and rewarding place than the Louvre. Sure, ya gotta see the *Mona Lisa* and *Venus de Milo,* but after you get your gottas out of the way, enjoy the Orsay.

ORIENTATION

Cost: €9, €6.50 Tue-Wed and Fri-Sun after 16:15 and Thu after 18:00, free first Sun of month, covered by Museum Pass. Tickets are good all day.

Hours: Tue-Sun 9:30-18:00, Thu until 21:45, closed Mon, last entry one hour before closing (45 minutes before on Thu). The top-floor Impressionist galleries begin closing 45 minutes early.

Free Entry near Closing Time: Right when the ticket booth stops selling tickets, visitors can often—but not always—scoot in free of charge (Tue-Wed and Fri-Sun at 17:00, Thu at 21:00; they won't let you in much after that, however). See the top floor first; it closes earliest.

Getting There: The museum is alongside the Seine River at 1 Rue de la Légion d'Honneur. It's well-connected by Métro (to Solférino), RER-C (Musée d'Orsay), bus #69, Batobus, and taxi. From the Louvre, it's a 15-minute walk through the Tuileries Garden and across the bridge.

Avoiding Lines: The ticket-buying line can be long, especially on Tue and Sun (it's least crowded Thu eve). But if you have a Museum Pass or advance ticket, you can waltz right in through Entrance C (to the right). Advance tickets can be purchased online (musee-orsay.fr) for a small surcharge and printed at home, or you can buy them in person at FNAC department stores and TIs.

Information: Tel. 01 40 49 48 14, musee-orsay.fr. The location of every painting is updated daily on the website: click "Collections," then "Interactive Floor Plan."

Tours: Audioguides cost €5. English guided tours usually run daily (except Sun) at 11:30 (€7.50/90 minutes). Or you can download a free Rick Steves **audio tour** (✪ see page 207).

Length of This Tour: Allow two hours.

Cloakroom (Vestiaire): Checking bags or coats is free. Day bags (but nothing bigger) are allowed in the museum. No valuables (cameras, passports, money) can be stored in checked bags.

Photography: It's forbidden.

Cuisine Art: The snazzy Le Restaurant on the second floor serves affordable tea and coffee (daily 15:00-17:30 except Thu). Less-pricey cafés are on the main floor and fifth floor. Outside, behind the museum, a number of classy eateries line Rue du Bac.

Starring: Manet, Monet, Renoir, Degas, Van Gogh, and Rodin.

Orsay Museum—Ground Floor

PONT ROYAL

Bus #69 *from Rue Cler to Louvre & Marais* Ⓑ

RUE DU BAC

Bus #69 from Marais to Rue Cler Ⓑ
To Louvre via Tuileries Garden (10 Min. Walk)

QUAI VOLTAIRE

ESCALATOR UP TO **IMPRESSIONISM**

Ⓑ *Batobus Boat Stop*

❼

❽

S e i n e   R i v e r

PLACE HENRY DE MONTHERLANT

MANET ❻

TOULOUSE-LAUTREC ❾

❺

❸

REALISM

CONSERVATIVE ART

RUE DE LILLE

❹ ❶ ❷

CAFE

BOOKSTORE

BOOKS

VESTIAIRE (BAGGAGE CHECK)

SECURITY

Bus #69 from Marais to Rue Cler & Eiffel Tower Ⓑ

QUAI ANATOLE FRANCE

Ⓣ

TICKET PURCHASERS →

ENTRANCE

← ADVANCE TICKET PASS HOLDERS

Ⓡ *Musee D'orsay*

Entrance Plaza

To Louvre via Tuileries Garden (15 Min. Walk)

RUE DE LA LEGION D'HONNEUR

RUE DE LA BELLECHASSE

SOLFERINO PEDESTRIAN BRIDGE

← To Orangerie (10 Min. Walk)

RUE DE SOLFERINO

To Ⓜ Solférino → (15 Min. Walk) & Rodin Museum

Not to Scale

❶ Main Gallery Statues

❷ INGRES – The Source

❸ DAUMIER – Celebrities of the Happy Medium

❹ MILLET – The Gleaners

❺ CABANEL – The Birth of Venus

❻ MANET – Olympia

❼ COURBET – The Painter's Studio

❽ Opéra Exhibit

❾ TOULOUSE-LAUTREC

The Orsay's main hall—former train station

Ingres' *Source*—clean, sculptural lines

THE TOUR BEGINS

Gare d'Orsay: The Old Train Station

▶ *Pick up a free English map upon entering, and check your bag. Belly up to the stone balustrade overlooking the main floor, and orient yourself.*

Trains used to run right under our feet down the center of the gallery. This former train station, or *gare,* barely escaped the wrecking ball in the 1970s, when the French realized it'd be a great place to house the enormous collections of 19th-century art scattered throughout the city.

The ground floor (Level 0) houses early 19th-century art, mainly conservative art and Realism. On the top floor (not visible from here) is the core of the collection—the Impressionist rooms. If you're pressed for time, go directly there. We'll start with conservatives and early rebels on the ground floor, then head upstairs to see how a few visionary young artists bucked the system and revolutionized the art world, paving the way for the 20th century. Clear as Seine water? *Bien.*

Remember that the museum rotates its large collection often, so find the latest arrangement on your current Orsay map, and be ready to go with the flow.

▶ *Walk down the steps to the main floor, a gallery filled with statues.*

CONSERVATIVE ART

Main Gallery Statues

No, this isn't ancient Greece. These statues arc from the same era as the Theory of Relativity. It's the Conservative art of the French schools, and it was very popular for its beauty—balanced poses, perfect anatomy, sweet faces, curving lines, and gleaming white stone. (I'll bad-mouth it later, but for now appreciate the exquisite craftsmanship of this "perfect" art.)

▶ *Take your first right into the small Room 1, marked* Ingres, Delacroix. *Look for a nude woman with a pitcher of water.*

Jean-Auguste-Dominique Ingres (1780-1867)—*The Source* (*La Source,* 1856)

Let's start where the Louvre left off. Ingres (ang-gruh, with a soft "gruh"), who helped cap the Louvre collection, championed a Neoclassical style. *The Source* is virtually a Greek statue on canvas. Her skin is porcelain-smooth, painted with seamless brushstrokes.

Ingres worked on this painting over the course of 35 years and considered it his "image of perfection." Famous in its day, *The Source*

The Orsay's "19th Century" (1848-1914)

Einstein and Geronimo. Abraham Lincoln and Karl Marx. The train, the bicycle, the horse and buggy, the automobile, and the balloon. Freud and Dickens. Darwin's *Origin of Species* and the Church's Immaculate Conception. Louis Pasteur and Billy the Kid. Ty Cobb and V. I. Lenin.

The 19th century was a mix of old and new, side by side. Europe was entering the modern Industrial Age, with cities, factories, rapid transit, instant communication, and global networks. At the same time, it clung to the past with traditional, rural—almost medieval—attitudes and morals.

According to the Orsay, the "19th century" began in 1848 with the socialist and democratic revolutions (Marx's *Communist Manifesto*). It ended in 1914 with the pull of an assassin's trigger, which ignited World War I and ushered in the modern world. The museum shows art that is also both old and new, conservative and revolutionary.

influenced many artists whose classical statues and paintings are in this museum.

In the Orsay's first few rooms, you're surrounded by visions of idealized beauty—nude women in languid poses, Greek mythological figures, and anatomically perfect statues. This was the art adored by French academics and the middle-class (*bourgeois*) public. The 19th-century art world was dominated by two conservative institutions: the Academy (the state-funded art school) and the Salon, where works were exhibited to the buying public. The art they produced was technically perfect, refined, uplifting, and heroic. Some might even say...boring.

▶ *Continue to Room 3 to find a pastel blue-green painting of a swooning Venus.*

Alexandre Cabanel (1823-1889)—*The Birth of Venus* (*La Naissance de Vénus,* 1863)

Cabanel lays Ingres' *The Source* on her back. This goddess is a perfect fantasy, an orgasm of beauty. The Love Goddess stretches back seductively, recently birthed from the ephemeral foam of the wave. This is art of a pre-Freudian society, when sex was dirty and mysterious and had to be exalted into a more pure and divine form. French folk would literally swoon in ecstasy before these works of art.

The public loved Cabanel's *Venus* (and Napoleon III purchased it). Like it? Go ahead, swoon. If it feels good, enjoy it. (If you feel guilty, get over it.) Now, take a mental cold shower and experience a Realist's take on the traditional Venus.

▶ *Cross the main gallery of statues, backtrack toward the entrance, and enter Room 4 (directly across from Ingres), marked Daumier.*

REALISM—EARLY REBELS

Honoré Daumier (1808-1879)—*Celebrities of the Happy Medium* (*Célébrités du Juste Milieu,* 1832-1835)

This is a liberal's look at the stuffy bourgeois establishment that controlled the Academy and the Salon. In these 36 bustlets, Daumier, trained as a political cartoonist, exaggerates each subject's most distinct characteristic to capture with vicious precision the pomposity and self-righteousness of these self-appointed arbiters of taste. The labels next to the busts give the

Cabanel's *Venus*—soft-porn fantasy   Millet's *Gleaners*—hard-core Realism

name of the person being caricatured, his title or job (most were members of the French parliament), and an insulting nickname (like "gross, fat, and satisfied" or Monsieur "Platehead"). Give a few nicknames yourself. Can you find Reagan, Clinton, Kerry, Sarkozy, Al Sharpton, and Gingrich?

These people hated the art you're about to see. Their prudish faces tightened as their fantasy world was shattered by the Realists.

▶ *Nearby (consult your free Orsay map to find it), you'll find...*

Jean-François Millet (1814-1875)—*The Gleaners* (*Les Glaneuses,* 1867)

Millet (mee yay) shows us three gleaners, the poor women who pick up the meager leftovers after a field has already been harvested by the wealthy. Millet grew up on a humble farm. He didn't attend the Academy and despised the uppity Paris art scene. Instead of idealized gods, goddesses, nymphs, and winged babies, he painted simple rural scenes. He was strongly affected by the socialist revolution of 1848, with its affirmation of the working class. Here he captures the innate dignity of these stocky, tanned women who bend their backs quietly in a large field for their small reward.

This is "Realism" in two senses. It's painted "realistically," unlike the prettified pastels of Cabanel's *Birth of Venus.* And it's the "real" world—not the fantasy world of Greek myth, but the harsh life of the working poor.

▶ *For a Realist's take on the traditional Venus, find Manet's* Olympia *in Room 14.*

Edouard Manet (1832-1883)—*Olympia* (1863)

"This brunette is thoroughly ugly. Her face is stupid, her skin cadaverous. All this clash of colors is stupefying." So wrote a critic when Edouard

Manet's *Olympia* shocked the public, mixing a classic pose with modern frankness.

Manet's nude hung in the Salon. The public hated it, attacking Manet (man-ay) in print and literally attacking the canvas.

Think back on Cabanel's painting, *The Birth of Venus:* an idealized, pastel, Vaseline-on-the-lens beauty. It's basically soft-core pornography, the kind you see today selling lingerie and perfume.

Manet's nude doesn't gloss over anything. The pose is classic, used by Titian, Goya, and countless others. But the traditional pose is challenged by the model's jarring frankness. The sharp outlines and harsh, contrasting colors are also new and shocking. Her hand is a clamp, and her stare is shockingly defiant, with not a hint of the seductive, hey-sailor look of most nudes. This prostitute, ignoring the flowers sent by her last customer, looks out as if to say, "Next." Manet replaced soft-core porn with hard-core art.

▶ *Make your way to the far left corner of Level 0, to a room called the Pavillon Amont, labeled* Courbet, grand formats. *It's dominated by a huge dark canvas...*

Gustave Courbet (1819-1877)—*The Painter's Studio* (*L'Atelier du Peintre,* 1855)

The Salon of 1855 rejected this dark-colored, sprawling, monumental painting of..."What's it about?" In an age when "Realist painter" was equated with "bomb-throwing Socialist," it took courage to buck the system.

Courbet—behind the scenes at his studio

"Grr. I hate Impressionism."

Dismissed by the so-called experts, Courbet (coor-bay) held his own one-man exhibit. He built a shed in the middle of Paris, defiantly hung his art out, and basically mooned the shocked public.

Courbet's painting takes us backstage, showing us the gritty reality behind the creation of pretty pictures. We see Courbet himself in his studio, working diligently on a Realistic landscape, oblivious to the confusion around him. Milling around are ordinary citizens, not Greek heroes. The woman who looks on is not a nude Venus but a naked artist's model. And the little boy with an adoring look on his face? Perhaps it's Courbet's inner child, admiring the artist who sticks to his guns, whether it's popular or not.

▶ *At the far end of the gallery, you'll walk on a glass floor over a model of Paris.*

Opéra Exhibit

Expand to 100 times your size and hover over this scale-model section of the city. In the center sits the 19th-century Opéra Garnier, with its green-domed roof. Nearby, you'll also see a cross-section model of the Opéra house and models of set designs from some famous productions. These days, Parisians enjoy their Verdi and Gounod at the modern opera house at Place de la Bastille.

The Opéra Garnier—opened in 1875—was the symbol of the belle époque, or "beautiful age." Paris was a global center of prosperity, new technology, opera, ballet, painting, and joie de vivre. But behind Paris' gilded and gas-lit exterior, a counterculture simmered.

▶ *For a taste of Parisian life during this golden (and not-so-golden) age, check out the Toulouse-Lautrec tucked away in Room 10, to the right of the Opéra exhibit.*

Henri de Toulouse-Lautrec (1864-1901)

Henri de Toulouse-Lautrec was the black sheep of a noble family. At age 14 he broke both legs, which left him with a normal-size torso but dwarf-size limbs. Shunned by his family, a freak to society, he felt more at home in the underworld of other outcasts—prostitutes, drunks, thieves, dancers, and actors. He settled in Montmartre, where he painted the life he lived. He drank absinthe and hung out with Van Gogh. He carried a hollow cane filled with booze. When the Moulin Rouge nightclub opened, Henri did their posters. Every night, the artist put on his bowler hat and visited the Moulin Rouge to draw the crowds, the can-can dancers, and the backstage action. Toulouse-Lautrec died at age 36 of syphilis and alcoholism.

Toulouse-Lautrec's painting style captures Realist scenes with strong, curvaceous outlines. He worked quickly, creating sketches in paint that serve as snapshots of a golden era. In *Jane Avril Dancing* (1891), he depicts the slim, graceful, elegant, and melancholy dancer, who stood out above the rabble. Her legs keep dancing while her mind is far away. Toulouse-Lautrec, the "artistocrat," might have identified with her noble face—sad and weary of the nightlife, but immersed in it.

▶ *Next up—the Orsay's Impressionist and Post-Impressionist collection. Take the escalator up to the top floor Impressionist rooms. Pause to take in a commanding view of the Orsay. Continue on past a bookshop and a giant "backward" clock (with great city views) to the art, starting in Room 29.*

The Impressionist collection is scattered somewhat randomly through Rooms 26-36. Shadows dance and the displays mingle. Where they're hung is a lot like their brushwork...delightfully sloppy. If you don't see a described painting, ask a guard or just move on. It's either hanging farther down or it's on vacation.

IMPRESSIONISM

Rooms 29-36: Manet, Degas, Monet, Renoir, and More

Light! Color! Vibrations! You don't hang an Impressionist canvas—you tether it. Impressionism features bright colors, easygoing open-air scenes, spontaneity, broad brushstrokes, and the play of light.

The Impressionists made their canvases shimmer by using a simple but revolutionary technique. Let's say you mix red, yellow, and green

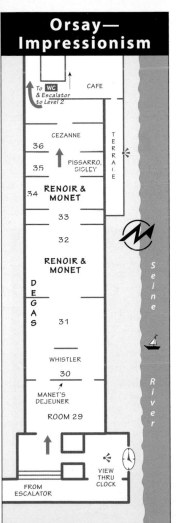

Orsay—
Impressionism

To WC
& Escalator
to Level 2

CAFE

CEZANNE

36

35

PISSARRO,
SISLEY

T
E
R
R
A
I
E

34

RENOIR &
MONET

33

32

RENOIR &
MONET

D
E
G
A
S

31

WHISTLER

30

MANET'S
DEJEUNER

ROOM 29

VIEW
THRU
CLOCK

FROM
ESCALATOR

S
e
i
n
e

R
i
v
e
r

together—you'll get brown, right? But Impressionists didn't bother to mix them. They'd slap a thick brushstroke of yellow down, then a stroke of green next to it, then red next to that. Up close, all you see are the three messy strokes, but as you back up... *voilà!* Brown! The colors blend in the eye, at a distance. But while your eye is saying, "bland old brown," your subconscious is shouting, "Red! Yellow! Green! Yes!"

There are no lines in nature, yet someone in the classical tradition (Ingres, for example) would draw an outline of his subject, then fill it in with color. Instead the Impressionists built a figure with dabs of paint...a snowman of color.

The artists labeled "Impressionists" were united by their commitment to everyday subjects (cafés, street scenes, landscapes, workers), their disdain for the uptight Salon, their love of color, and a sense of artistic rebellion.

▶ *Remember, the following tour is less a room-by-room itinerary than an introduction to the Orsay's ever-changing collection. Have fun exploring: Think of it as a sun-dappled treasure hunt.*

Edouard Manet (1832-1883)— Luncheon on the Grass (Le Déjeuner sur l'Herbe, 1863)

A shocked public looked at this and wondered: What are these scantily clad women doing with these men? Or rather, what will they be doing after the last baguette is eaten? It isn't the nudity, but the presence of the men in ordinary clothes, that suddenly makes the nudes look naked. Once again, the public judged the painting on moral rather than artistic terms.

A new revolutionary movement was starting to bud—Impressionism. Notice the background: the messy brushwork of trees and leaves, the play of light on the pond, and the light that filters through the trees onto the woman who stoops in the haze. Also note the strong contrast of colors (white skin, black clothes, green grass). This is a true out-of-doors painting, not a studio production.

Edouard Manet became the leader of the Impressionist group, though he learned equally from his peers. (You may see paintings by Henri Fantin-Latour, showing a group of business-suited Impressionists.) Manet's thumbnail bio is typical of almost all the Impressionists: They rejected a "normal" career (lawyer, banker, grocer) to become artists, got classical

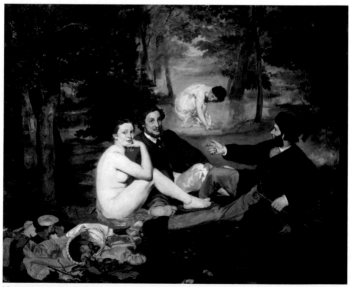

Manet, the mentor of the Impressionists, experimented with open-air painting.

Painting "in the Open Air"

The camera threatened to make artists obsolete. Now a machine could capture a better likeness faster than you could say "Etch-a-Sketch."

But true art is more than just painting reality. It gives us reality from the artist's point of view, with the artist's personal impressions of the scene. Impressions are often fleeting, so working quickly is essential.

The Impressionist painters rejected camera-like detail for a quick style more suited to capturing the passing moment. Feeling stifled by the rigid rules and stuffy atmosphere of the Academy, the Impressionists grabbed their berets and scarves and went on excursions to the country. They set up their easels (and newly invented tubes of premixed paint) on riverbanks and hillsides, or they sketched in cafés and dance halls. Gods, goddesses, nymphs, and fantasy scenes were out; common people and rural landscapes were in.

The quick style and everyday subjects were ridiculed and called childish by the "experts." They brashly took their name from an insult thrown at them by a critic who laughed at one of Monet's "impressions" of a sunrise. Rejected by the Salon, the Impressionists staged their own exhibition in 1874. The public, opposed at first, was slowly won over by the simplicity, color, and vibrancy of Impressionist art.

art training, exhibited in the Salon, became fascinated by Realist subjects, and grew tired of the Salon's dogmatism. They joined the Impressionist exhibition of 1874, experimented with bright colors and open-air scenes, and moved on to forge their unique styles in later years.

Let the Impressionist revolution begin.

▶ *Among the colorful Impressionist works, find the non-Impressionist but equally famous...*

James Abbott McNeill Whistler (1834-1903) — *Portrait of the Artist's Mother* (*Portrait de la Mère de l'Auteur,* 1871)

Why's it so famous? I don't know either. Perhaps because it's by an American, and we see in his mother some of the monumental solidity of our own ancestral moms, who were made tough by pioneering the American wilderness.

Or perhaps because it was so starkly different for its day. In a room-ful of golden goddesses, it'd stand out like a fish in a tree. The alternate title is *Arrangement in Gray and Black, No. 1,* and the whole point is the subtle variations of dark shades softened by the rosy tint of her cheeks. Nevertheless, the critics kept waiting for it to come out in Colorization.

▶ *In the next couple of rooms, find works by Edgar Degas.*

Edgar Degas (1834-1917)

Clearly, Degas loved dance and the theater. (Catch his statue, *Tiny Dancer, 14 Years Old,* in the glass case.) The play of stage lights off his dancers, especially the halos of ballet skirts, is made to order for an Impressionist. In *The Dance Class,* bored, tired dancers scratch their backs restlessly at the end of a long rehearsal. And look at the bright green bow on the girl with her back to us. In the Impressionist style, Degas slopped green paint onto her dress and didn't even say, *"Excusez-moi."*

Edgar Degas (day-gah) was a rich kid from a family of bankers, and he got the best classical-style art training. He painted in the Academic style, exhibited in the Salon, gained a good reputation, and then...he met the Impressionists.

Degas combined Ingres' classical lines and Realist subjects with Impressionist color, spontaneity, and everyday subjects from urban Paris. Degas loved the unposed "snapshot" effect, catching his models off guard. Dance students, women at work, and café scenes are approached from odd angles that aren't always ideal, but make the scenes seem more real. He gives us the backstage view of life.

Whistler's *Mother*—50 shades of gray

Degas—Behind the scenes look at dancers

Degas took "snapshots" of ordinary people—at work, at the theater, or in a late-night café.

In **The Glass of Absinthe** (*Au Café, dit L'Absinthe, 1876*) a weary lady of the evening meets morning with a last, lonely, nail-in-the-coffin drink in the glaring light of a four-in-the-morning café. The pale green drink at the center of the composition is the toxic substance absinthe, which fueled many artists and burned out many more.

▶ *Scattered all around you are works by two Impressionist masters at their peak, Monet and Renoir. You're looking at the quintessence of Impressionism. The two were good friends, often working side-by-side, and their canvases sometimes hang side-by-side in these rooms.*

Claude Monet (1840-1926)

Monet (mo-nay) is the father of Impressionism. He fully explored the possibilities of open-air painting and tried to faithfully reproduce nature's colors with bright blobs of paint. Throughout his long career, more than any of his colleagues, Monet stuck to the Impressionist credo of creating objective studies in color and light.

In the 1860s, Monet (along with Renoir) began painting landscapes in the open air. Although Monet did the occasional urban scene, he was most at home in the countryside, painting farms, rivers, trees, and passing clouds. He studied optics and pigments to know just the right colors he needed to reproduce the shimmering quality of reflected light. The key was to work quickly—at that "golden hour" (to use a modern cinematographer's term), when the light was just right. Then he'd create a fleeting "impression" of the scene.

Claude Monet—*The Cathedral of Rouen* (*La Cathédrale de Rouen,* 1893)

In 1893, Monet went to Rouen, rented a room across from the cathedral, set up his easel...and waited. He wanted to catch "a series of differing impressions" of the cathedral facade at various times of day and year. He often had several canvases going at once. In all, he did 30 paintings of the cathedral, and each is unique. The time-lapse series shows the sun passing slowly across the sky, creating different-colored light and shadows. The labels next to the art describe the conditions: in gray weather, in the morning, morning sun, full sunlight, and so on.

As Monet zeroes in on the play of colors and light, the physical subject—the cathedral—is dissolving. It's only a rack upon which to hang the light and color. Later artists would boldly throw away the rack, leaving purely abstract modern art in its place.

Claude Monet—Paintings from Monet's Garden at Giverny

One of Monet's favorite places to paint was the garden he landscaped at his home in Giverny, west of Paris (and worth a visit, provided you like Monet more than you hate crowds). The Japanese bridge and the water lilies floating in the pond were his two favorite subjects. As Monet aged and his eyesight failed, he made bigger canvases of smaller subjects. The final water lilies (at the Orangerie and Marmottan museums) are monumental smudges of thick paint surrounded by paint-splotched clouds reflected on the surface of the pond.

Pierre-Auguste Renoir (1841-1919)

Renoir (ren-wah) started out as a painter of landscapes, along with Monet, but later veered from the Impressionist's philosophy and painted images that were unabashedly "pretty." He populated his canvases with rosy-cheeked, middle-class girls performing happy domestic activities,

Monet's cathedral dissolves into a pattern of paint, pointing the way toward purely abstract art.

rendered in a warm, inviting style. As Renoir himself said, "There are enough ugly things in life."

Renoir's lighthearted work uses light colors—no brown or black. The paint is thin and translucent, and the outlines are soft, so the figures blend seamlessly with the background. He seems to be searching for an ideal, the sort of pure beauty we saw in paintings on the ground floor.

In his last years (when he was confined to a wheelchair with arthritis), Renoir turned to full-figured nudes—like those painted by Old Masters such as Rubens or Boucher. He introduced more and more red tones, as if trying for even greater warmth.

Pierre-Auguste Renoir—*Dance at the Moulin de la Galette* (*Bal du Moulin de la Galette,* 1876)

On Sunday afternoons, working-class folk would dress up and head for the fields on Butte Montmartre (near Sacré-Cœur basilica) to dance, drink,

Renoir—in this scene from Montmartre—captures the joie de vivre of the belle époque.

and eat little crêpes *(galettes)* till dark. Renoir liked to go there to paint the common Parisians living and loving in the afternoon sun. The sunlight filtering through the trees creates a kaleidoscope of colors, like the 19th-century equivalent of a mirror ball throwing darts of light onto the dancers.

He captures the dappled light with quick blobs of yellow staining the ground, the men's jackets, and the sun-dappled straw hat (right of center). Smell the powder on the ladies' faces. The painting glows with bright colors. Even the shadows on the ground, which should be gray or black, are colored a warm blue. Like a photographer who uses a slow shutter speed to show motion, Renoir paints a waltzing blur.

▶ *Before moving on, check out some of the "lesser" pioneers of the Impressionist style—Pissarro, Sisley, and others. A café is up ahead, and WCs are nearby. You deserve a break.*

POST-IMPRESSIONISM

Post-Impressionism—the style that employs Impressionism's bright colors while branching out in new directions—is scattered all around the museum. Start here on the top floor with Paul Cézanne, who many consider to be one of the founders of Modern art.

Paul Cézanne (1839-1906)

Paul Cézanne (say-zahn) brought Impressionism into the 20th century. Compared with the colors of Monet, the warmth of Renoir, and Van Gogh's passion, Cézanne's rather impersonal canvases can be difficult to appreciate. Bowls of fruit, landscapes, and a few portraits were Cézanne's passion. Because of his style (not his content), he is often called the first modern painter.

Cézanne was born in Provence, and shuttled between Paris and the south of France all his life. Although he exhibited with the Impressionists, he preferred his home ground, painting the rocky, arid Provençal landscape. Cézanne was virtually unknown and unappreciated in his lifetime, ignored by all but a few revolutionary young artists who understood his efforts.

Unlike the Impressionists, who painted what they saw, Cézanne reworked reality. He simplified it into basic geometric forms—circular apples, rectangular boulders, cone-shaped trees, triangular groups of people.

He might depict a scene from multiple angles—showing a table-top from above and the bowl of fruit on top of the table from the side. He laid paint with heavy brushstrokes, blending the background and foreground to obliterate traditional 3-D depth. He worked slowly, methodically, stroke by stroke—a single canvas could take months.

Cezanne—*The Card Players* (*Les Joueurs de Cartes*, c. 1890-1895)

These aren't people. They're studies in color and pattern. The subject matter—two guys playing cards—is less important than the pleasingly balanced pattern they make on the canvas, two sloping forms framing a cylinder (a bottle) in the center. Later, abstract artists would focus solely on shapes and colors.

Whereas the Impressionists built a figure out of a mosaic of individual brushstrokes, Cézanne used chunky patches of paint. The jackets are a patchwork of tans, greens, and browns. Even the "empty" space between

Cezanne built this scene out of patches of paint, anticipating the "cubes" of Cubism.

the men—painted with fragmented chunks of color—is almost as tangible as they are. As one art scholar puts it: "Cézanne confused intermingled forms and colors, achieving an extraordinarily luminous density in which lyricism is controlled by a rigorously constructed rhythm." Just what I said—chunks of color.

The chunks could also be called "cubes." It's no coincidence that his experiments in reducing forms to their geometric basics influenced the... Cubists.

▶ *You'll find more Post-Impressionists on Level 2. To get there from the café, find the escalators (the ones going down) and descend to Level 2. Go along the right side of the open-air mezzanine, where you'll find the entrance to the darkened Room 72, the first of several rooms with works by Van Gogh and Gauguin.*

Vincent van Gogh (1853-1890)

Impressionists have been accused of being "light"-weights. The colorful style lends itself to bright country scenes, gardens, sunlight on the water, and happy crowds of simple people. It took a remarkable genius to add profound emotion to the Impressionist style.

Like Michelangelo, Beethoven, Rembrandt, Wayne Newton, and a select handful of others, Vincent van Gogh (pronounced van-go, or van-HOCK by the Dutch and the snooty) put so much of himself into his work that art and life became one. In the Orsay's collection of paintings, you'll see both Van Gogh's painting style and his life unfold.

Vincent van Gogh—*Peasant Woman near the Hearth* (*Paysanne près de l'Atre,* 1885)

As the son of a Dutch minister, Van Gogh feels drawn to a religious vocation, and he spreads the gospel among the poorest of the poor—peasants and miners in overcast Holland and Belgium. He paints these hardworking, dignified folks in a crude, dark style that reflects the oppressiveness of their lives...and the loneliness of his own as he roams northern Europe in search of a calling.

Vincent van Gogh—*Self-Portrait, Paris* (*Portrait de l'Artiste,* 1887)

Encouraged by his art-dealer brother, Van Gogh moves to Paris, and *voilà!* The color! He meets Monet, drinks with Paul Gauguin and Henri de Toulouse-Lautrec, and soaks up the Impressionist style. (See how he

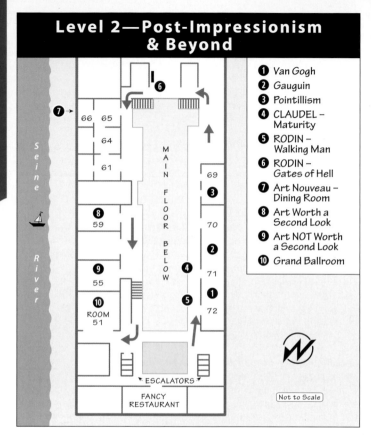

Level 2—Post-Impressionism & Beyond

1. Van Gogh
2. Gauguin
3. Pointillism
4. CLAUDEL – Maturity
5. RODIN – Walking Man
6. RODIN – Gates of Hell
7. Art Nouveau – Dining Room
8. Art Worth a Second Look
9. Art NOT Worth a Second Look
10. Grand Ballroom

Seine River

MAIN FLOOR BELOW

66 65
64
61
59
55
ROOM 51
69
70
71
72

ESCALATORS

FANCY RESTAURANT

Not to Scale

builds a bristling brown beard using thick strokes of red, yellow, and green side-by-side.)

At first, he paints like the others, but soon he develops his own style. By using thick, swirling brushstrokes, he even infuses life into inanimate objects. Van Gogh's brushstrokes curve and thrash like a garden hose pumped full of wine.

In Van Gogh's *Self-Portrait,* the swirl of brushstrokes captures the artist's restless energy.

Vincent van Gogh—*Midday*
(*La Méridienne,* 1890, based on a painting by Millet)

The social life of Paris becomes too much for the solitary Van Gogh. He moves to the South of France. At first, in the glow of the bright spring sunshine, he has a period of incredible creativity and happiness, as he is overwhelmed by the bright colors, landscape vistas, and common people—an Impressionist's dream.

Vincent van Gogh—*Van Gogh's Room at Arles*
(*La Chambre de van Gogh à Arles,* 1889)

But being alone in a strange country begins to wear on him. An ugly man, he finds it hard to get a date. The close-up perspective of this painting makes his tiny, rented room look even more cramped. He invites his friend Gauguin to join him, but after two months together arguing passionately

Van Gogh's Room at Arles

The mysterious *Church at Auvers-sur-Oise*

about art, nerves get raw. Van Gogh threatens Gauguin with a knife, and in crazed despair, mutilates his own ear.

The people of Arles realize they have a madman on their hands and convince Van Gogh to seek help. He enters a mental hospital.

Vincent van Gogh—*The Church at Auvers-sur-Oise* (*L'Eglise d'Auvers-sur-Oise,* 1890)

Van Gogh's paintings done in the peace of the mental hospital are more meditative—fewer bright landscapes, more closed-in scenes with deeper and almost surreal colors. Van Gogh, the preacher's son, saw painting as a calling, and he approached it with a spiritual intensity.

The sky is cobalt blue and the church's windows are also blue, as if we're looking right through the building to an infinite sky. There's a road that leads from us to the church, then splits to go behind it. A choice must be made: which way?

Vincent van Gogh—*Self-Portrait, St. Rémy* (1889)

Van Gogh wavers between happiness and madness. He despairs of ever being sane enough to continue painting.

This self-portrait shows a man engulfed in a confused background of brushstrokes that swirl and rave, setting in motion the waves of the jacket. But in the midst of this rippling sea of mystery floats a still, detached island of a face with a probing, questioning, wise expression.

Do his troubled eyes know that only a few months on, he will take a pistol and put a bullet through his chest? Vincent van Gone.

▶ *Also in Rooms 70-72, look for...*

Paul Gauguin (1848-1903)

Paul Gauguin (go-gan) got the travel bug early in childhood and grew up wanting to be a sailor. Instead, he became a stockbroker. In his spare time, he painted, and he was introduced to the Impressionist circle. At 35, he quit his job, abandoned his wife (her stern portrait bust may be nearby), and traveled to the South Seas in search of the exotic.

In Tahiti, Gauguin found his Garden of Eden. He simplified his life into a routine of eating, sleeping, and painting. He painted the native girls in their naked innocence (so different from Cabanel's seductive *Venus*). His simple paintings feature flat images with heavy black outlines filled with bright, pure colors. The background and foreground colors are equally bright, producing a flat, stained-glass-like surface.

Gauguin—*Arearea*, or *Joyousness* (*Joyeusetés*, 1892)

Here is the paradise Gauguin always envisioned. It's an idyllic landscape

Gauguin paints his primitive paradise, using childlike blocks of bright color.

peopled by exotic women engaged in simple tasks and making music. A lazy dog dominates the foreground. The style is intentionally "primitive," collapsing the three-dimensional landscape into a two-dimensional pattern of bright colors.

This simple style had a deep undercurrent of symbolic meaning. In the distance, women bow down to a large pagan idol. What's the connection between the idol and the foreground figures? In primitive societies, religion permeates life. Idols, dogs, and women are equally holy.

▶ *Next, in Room 69, find several* **Pointillist paintings.** *This style brings Impressionism to its logical conclusion—little dabs of different colors placed side by side to blend in the viewer's eye. The essential Orsay includes one final artist—the sculptor Rodin, whose work is located along the open-air mezzanine of Level 2—some near Room 72, others at the far end.*

Auguste Rodin (1840-1917)

Born of working-class roots and largely self-taught, Rodin (ro-dan) combined classical solidity with Impressionist surfaces to become the greatest sculptor since Michelangelo. He labored in obscurity for decades, making knickknacks and doorknobs for a construction company. By age 40, he started to gain recognition. He became romantically involved with a student, Camille Claudel, who became his model and muse.

Rodin's subject was always the human body, showing it in unusual poses to express inner emotion. The surface is alive, rippling with frosting-like gouges.

The style comes from Rodin's work process. Rodin paid models to run, squat, leap, and spin around his studio however they wanted. When he saw an interesting pose, he'd yell, "Freeze!" (or "Statue maker") and get out his sketchpad. Rodin worked quickly, using his powerful thumbs to make a small statue in clay, which he would then reproduce as a life-size clay statue that, in turn, was used as a mold for casting a plaster or bronze copy. Authorized copies of Rodin's work are now included in museums all over the world.

▶ *Start with the man missing everything but his legs.*

Auguste Rodin—*The Walking Man* (*L'Homme Qui Marche,* c. 1900)

Like this statue, Auguste Rodin had one foot in the past, while the

Rodin worked in bronze, so there are authorized versions of this work elsewhere.

other was stepping into the future. Rodin combined classical solidity with Impressionist surfaces to become the greatest sculptor since Michelangelo.

This muscular, forcefully striding man could be a symbol of Renaissance Man with his classical power. With no mouth or hands, he speaks with his body. Get close and look at the statue's surface. This rough, "unfinished" look reflects light in the same way the rough Impressionist brushwork does, making the statue come alive, never quite at rest in the viewer's eye.

▶ *Also along the mezzanine, you'll see a small bronze statue of a couple.*

Camille Claudel—*Maturity* (*L'Age Mûr,* 1899-1903)

Camille Claudel, Rodin's student and mistress, may have portrayed their doomed love affair here. A young girl desperately reaches out to an older man, who is led away reluctantly by an older woman. The center of the composition is the empty space left when their hands separate. In real life, Rodin refused to leave his wife, and Claudel (see her head sticking up from a block of marble nearby) ended up in an insane asylum.

▶ *Continue along the mezzanine to the far end, where you'll find...*

Auguste Rodin—*The Gates of Hell* (*La Porte de l'Enfer,* 1880-1917)

Rodin worked for decades on these doors depicting Dante's hell, and they contain some of his greatest hits—small statues that he later executed in full size. Find *The Thinker* squatting above the doorway, contemplating Man's fate. And in the lower left is the same kneeling man eating his children *(Ugolin)* that you'll see in full size nearby.

From this perch, look over the main floor at the classical statues

Claudel was dumped by Rodin.

Salle des Fêtes (Grand Ballroom)

below—beautiful, smooth, balanced, and idealized—and realize how far we've come. Rodin's powerful, haunting works capture the groundbreaking spirit of much of the art in the Orsay Museum. With a stable base of 19th-century stone, he launched art into the 20th century.

▶ *You've seen the essential Orsay and are permitted to cut out. But if you have extra time, there's an "other" Orsay you may find interesting. The beauty of the Orsay is that it combines all the art from 1848 to 1914, both modern and classical, in one building. Rooms 61-66 are a curvaceous IKEA of Art Nouveau furniture. Rooms 55 and 59 feature some non-Impressionist art—so popular in the 19th century and now so unpopular. The chandeliered Salle des Fêtes (Grand Ballroom, Room 51) was once one of Paris' poshest nightspots.*

Finish with a slice of opulent, fin de siècle Paris at the still-functioning Le Restaurant, located near the escalators on Level 2. After all this art, you deserve it.

One last look—at the main floor, the mezzanine, and the great art we've seen on this tour

Eiffel Tower Tour

La Tour Eiffel

It's crowded, expensive, and there are probably better views in Paris, but visiting this 1,000-foot-tall ornament is worth the trouble. Visitors to Paris may find *Mona Lisa* to be less than expected, but the Eiffel Tower rarely disappoints, even in an era of skyscrapers. This is a once-in-a-lifetime, I've-been-there experience. Making the trip gives you membership in the exclusive society of the quarter of a billion other humans who have made the Eiffel Tower the most visited monument in the modern world.

Reserve an entry time well in advance, and follow my other crowd-beating tips. Then relax and enjoy one of the most breathtaking 1,000-foot journeys in the world.

ORIENTATION

Cost: €14.50 all the way to the top, €8.50 if you're only going up to the two lower levels, not covered by Museum Pass. You can skip the elevator line and climb the stairs to the first and second level for €5; it's another €5.50 to take the elevator from the second level to the top.

Hours: Open daily mid-June-Aug 9:00-24:45, last ascent to top at 23:00 and to lower levels at 24:00; Sept-mid-June 9:30-23:45, last ascent to top at 22:30 and to lower levels at 23:00 (elevator). Access to the stairs closes at 18:00 in off-season.

Reservations and Avoiding Lines: There are generally one- to two-hour waits to get in. Weekends and holidays are worst; rainy days are least crowded.

At tour-eiffel.fr, you can book an entry time (e.g., 12 June at 16:30) and skip the line—at no extra cost. You pay online, print your own ticket (or have it sent to your mobile phone), and enter the tower at the entrance for *visitors with reservation*. Note that, even with a prepaid reservation, to catch the elevator from the second level to the summit, you'll still have to wait in line like everybody else. Reserve months in advance for summer visits. If it's all booked up, try the website again a week before you arrive, or look for "2nd level" tickets.

Without a reservation, try arriving first thing in the morning or later in the day (after 19:00 May-Aug, after 17:00 off-season), or take the (less-crowded) stairs. To avoid lines for the elevator to the top level, you could content yourself with the still-fine views from the second level. A reservation at either of the tower's view restaurants lets you skip the worst lines (see "Eating," next page). Classicwalks.com sells €40 last-minute reservations.

When to Go: For the best of both worlds, arrive with enough light to see the views, then stay as it gets dark to see the lights.

Getting There: The Bir-Hakeim and Trocadéro Métro stops, and the Champ de Mars-Tour Eiffel RER stop, are each about a 10-minute walk away. The Ecole Militaire Métro stop in the Rue Cler area is 20 minutes away. Buses #69 and #87 stop nearby.

Information: Information offices are between the north and east pillars and at the west pillar, next to the Group Desk. Tel. 01 44 11 23 23, tour-eiffel.fr.

Length of This Tour: With a reservation and minimal crowds, figure 90 minutes to the top and back. It takes three or four hours with crowds and lines.

Pickpockets: In crowded elevators and lines, *en garde.*

Security Check: Bags larger than 19" × 8" × 12" are not allowed, and there is no baggage check. All bags are subject to a security search. No knives, glass bottles, or cans are allowed.

Services: There are free WCs at the base of the tower behind the east pillar. Inside the tower itself, WCs are on all levels, but they have long lines.

Photography: All photos and videos are allowed.

Eating: The first and second levels have small sandwich-and-pizza-type cafés (€5), and the first level occasionally has temporary "pop-up" restaurants.

The tower's two classy restaurants offer great views, and a reservation at either restaurant lets you skip the initial elevator line. Reserve far in advance for a view table, especially at dinner. On the first level is 58 Tour Eiffel (€40 lunches; walk-ins welcome, €75-165 dinners, open daily, tel. 01 72 76 18 46, restaurants-toureiffel.com). The expensive Jules Verne Restaurant is on the second level (€90 lunch *menu,* €210 dinner *menu,* open daily, tel. 01 45 55 61 44, lejulesverne-paris.com).

At the tower's base, there's not much besides the burger-and-fries stands. Rue Cler, with many options, is a 20-minute walk away (❂ see pages 188-189). Avenue de la Bourdonnais, a mere block east of the tower, has a few eateries and sandwich shops, including Pâtisserie de la Tour Eiffel, which offers inexpensive salads, quiche,

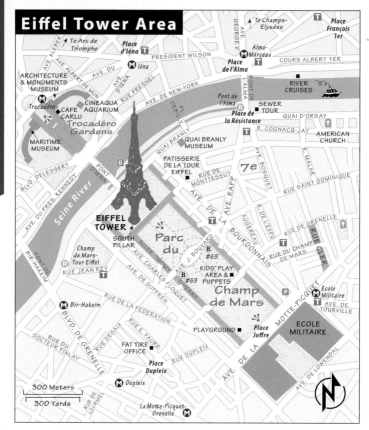

Eiffel Tower Area

sandwiches, and tower views (21 Avenue de la Bourdonnais, tel. 01 47 05 59 81).

Your tastiest option may be to assemble a picnic beforehand to eat alongside the Champ de Mars park. The center of the park is off-limits to picnickers.

Starring: All of Paris...and beyond.

THE TOUR BEGINS

There are three observation platforms, at 200, 400, and 900 feet. Although being on the windy top of the Eiffel Tower is a thrill you'll never forget, the view is better from the first and second levels, where you can actually see Paris' monuments. All three levels have some displays, WCs (usually with long lines), souvenir stores, and a few other services.

To get to the top, you need to ride one elevator to the second level, then catch a second elevator to the top. For the hardy, stairs lead from the ground level up to the first level (360 steps) and second level (another 360 steps). The staircase is enclosed with a wire cage, so you can't fall, but those with vertigo issues may still find them dizzying.

If you want to see the entire tower, from top to bottom, then see it... from top to bottom. Ride the elevator to the second level (if your elevator stops at the first level on the way up, don't get off), then immediately line up for the other elevator to the top. Enjoy the views on top, then ride back down to the second level. Frolic there for a while, then descend to the first level via the stairs (no line) or elevator (before boarding, ask if the elevator will stop on the first level—some don't). After more views, shops, exhibits, and a snack, take the elevator or stairs back down to earth.

▶ *Find the various entrances at the base of the tower's four* piliers *(pillars), named for their compass points:* nord, sud, est, and ouest. *Make sure you get in the right line. If you have a reservation, look for signs saying* visitors with reservation. *Otherwise, follow signs for* individuels *or* visiteurs sans tickets. *(Avoid lines selling tickets only for* groupes.*) To climb the stairs, enter at the south pillar, next to the Jules Verne Restaurant entrance. As you wait to enter, look up at the tower towering above you, and don't even think about what would happen if someone dropped a coin from the top.*

Exterior

Delicate and graceful when seen from afar, the Eiffel Tower is massive— even a bit scary—close up. You don't appreciate its size until you walk toward it; like a mountain, it seems so close but takes forever to reach.

The tower, including its antenna, stands 1,063 feet tall, or slightly higher than the 77-story Chrysler Building in New York. Its four support pillars straddle an area of 3.5 acres. Despite the tower's 7,300 tons of metal

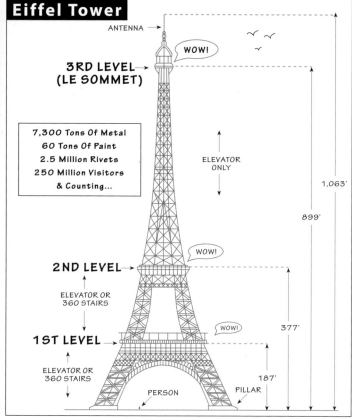

Eiffel Tower

ANTENNA →

WOW!

3RD LEVEL →
(LE SOMMET)

7,300 Tons Of Metal
60 Tons Of Paint
2.5 Million Rivets
250 Million Visitors
& Counting...

ELEVATOR
ONLY

1,063'

899'

WOW!

2ND LEVEL →

ELEVATOR OR
360 STAIRS

WOW!

377'

1ST LEVEL →

ELEVATOR OR
360 STAIRS

187'

PERSON

PILLAR

and 60 tons of paint, it is so well-engineered that it weighs no more per square inch at its base than a linebacker on tiptoes.

Once the world's tallest structure, it's now eclipsed by a number of towers (e.g., the CN Tower, Toronto, 1,815 feet), radio antennae (KVLY-TV Mast, North Dakota, 2,063 feet), and skyscrapers (the Burj Khalifa in Dubai, UAE, 2,717 feet, and Sky City in Changsha, China, 2,749 feet).

Eiffel—designer, financier, and builder

Wheels turn cables to lift the elevator.

The long green lawn stretching south of the tower is the Champ de Mars, originally the training ground for troops and students of the nearby Military School (Ecole Militaire) and now a park. On the north side, across the Seine, is the curved palace colonnade framing a square called the Trocadéro, site of numerous world's fairs.

History

In 1889, the first visitor to Paris' Universal Exposition walked beneath the "arch" formed by the newly built Eiffel Tower and entered the fairgrounds. The World's Fair celebrated both the centennial of the French Revolution and France's position as a global superpower. Bridge-builder Gustave Eiffel (1832-1923) won the contest to build the fair's centerpiece by beating out such rival proposals as a giant guillotine.

Gustave deserved to have the tower named for him. He not only designed it, he financed it, his factory produced the iron beams, he invented special cranes and apparatus, he paid the workers, and—working on a deadline for the World's Fair—he brought in the project on time and under budget.

The tower was nothing but a showpiece, with no functional purpose except to demonstrate to the world that France had the wealth, knowledge, and can-do spirit to erect a structure far taller than anything the world had ever seen. The original plan was to dismantle the tower as quickly as it was built after the celebration ended, but it was kept by popular demand.

To a generation hooked on technology, the tower was the marvel of the age, a symbol of progress and human ingenuity. Not all were so impressed, however; many found it a monstrosity. The writer Guy de

Building the Tower

As you ascend through the metal beams, imagine being a worker, perched high above nothing, riveting this thing together. It was a massive project, and it took all the ingenuity of the Industrial Age—including mass production, cutting-edge technology, and capitalist funding.

An 18,000-piece Erector set

The tower went up like an 18,000-piece erector set, made of 15-foot iron beams held together with 2.5 million rivets. For two years, 300 workers assembled the pieces, the tower rising as they went.

First, they sank massive iron pillars into the ground at an angle, surrounded by cement 20 feet thick and capped with stone. They erected wooden scaffolding to support the lower (angled) sections,

Maupassant (1850-1893) routinely ate lunch in the tower just so he wouldn't have to look at it.

In subsequent years, the tower has come to serve many functions: as a radio transmitter (1909-present), a cosmic-ray observatory (1910), a billboard (spelling "Citroën" in lights, 1925-1934), a broadcaster of Nazi TV programs (1940-1944), a fireworks launch pad (numerous times), and as a framework for dazzling lighting displays, including the current arrangement, designed in 2000 for the celebration of the millennium.

▶ *To reach the top, ride the elevator or walk to the second level. From there, get in line for the next elevator and continue to the top. Pop out 900 feet above the ground.*

Third Level (*Le Sommet,* or Summit)

The top level is tiny. All you'll find here are wind and grand, sweeping views. The city lies before you, with a panorama guide. On a good day, you can until the pillars came together and the tower could support itself. Then the iron beams were lifted up with steam-powered cranes, including cranes on tracks (creeper cranes) that inched up the pillars as the tower progressed. There, daring workers dangled from rope ladders, balanced on beams, and tightrope-walked their way across them as they put the pieces in place. The workers then hammered in red-hot rivets which, as they cooled, locked the structure in place.

After a mere year and a half of work, the tower already surpassed the previous tallest building in the world—the Washington Monument (555 feet)—which had taken 36 years to build.

The tower was painted a rusty red. Since then, it's sported several colors, including mustard and the current brown-gray. It is repainted every seven years, a process that takes 25 full-time painters 18 months to apply 60 tons of paint by hand—no spraying allowed.

Two years, two months, and five days after construction began, the tower was done. On May 15, 1889, a red, white, and blue beacon was lit on the top, the World's Fair began, and the tower carried its first astounded visitor to the top.

see for 40 miles. Do a 360-degree tour of Paris. (Note that the following compass points are only approximate; in fact, what the tower's displays call "west" is more like southwest, etc.) Feeling proud you made it this high? You can celebrate your accomplishment with a €10 glass of champagne.

Looking West *(Ouest):* The Seine runs east to west (though at this point it's flowing more southwest). At the far end of the skinny "island" in the river, find the tiny copy of the Statue of Liberty, looking 3,633 miles away to her big sister in New York. Gustave Eiffel, a man of many talents, also designed the internal supports of New York's Statue of Liberty, which was cast in copper by fellow Frenchman Frederic Bartholdi (1886).

Looking North *(Nord):* At your feet is the curved arcade of the Trocadéro. Beyond that is the vast, forested expanse of the Bois de Boulogne, the three-square-mile park that hosts joggers and *boules* players by day and prostitutes by night. In the far distance are the skyscrapers of La Défense, and to the right of the Trocadéro is the Arc de Triomphe.

Looking west—next stop, New York

Looking north—Place Trocadéro

Looking East (Est): At your feet are the Seine and its many bridges, including Pont Alexandre, with its four golden statues. Looking farther upstream, find the Orsay Museum, the Louvre, Pont Neuf, and the twin towers of Notre-Dame.

In the far distance on the Right Bank is the bullet-shaped dome of Sacré-Cœur, atop Butte Montmartre.

Looking South (Sud): In a line, find the Champ de Mars, the Ecole Militaire, the Y-shaped UNESCO building, and the 689-foot Montparnasse Tower skyscraper. To the left is the golden dome of Les Invalides.

The Tippy Top: Ascend another short staircase to the open-air top, beneath satellite dishes. You'll see the tiny apartment given to the builder of the tower. The mannequins re-create the moment during the 1889 Exhibition when the American Thomas Edison paid a visit to his fellow techie, Gustave Eiffel (the one with the beard) and Gustave's daughter Claire, presenting them with his new invention, a phonograph. (Then they cranked it up and blasted The Who's "I Can See for Miles.")

▶ *Catch the elevator down to the...*

Second Level

The second level (400 feet) has the best views because you're closer to the sights, and the monuments are more recognizable. This level has souvenir shops, public telephones to call home, and a small stand-up café.

The famous Jules Verne Restaurant on this level is currently run by celebrity chef Alain Ducasse. One would hope his brand of haute cuisine matches the 400-foot haute of the restaurant.

▶ *Catch the elevator or take the stairs (5 minutes, 360 steps, free) down to the...*

Up and Down

The tower—which was designed from the start to accommodate hordes of visitors—has always had elevators. Back in the late 19th century, elevator technology was so new that they needed a special design to accommodate the angle of the tower's pillars. Today's elevators (modern replacements) make about 100 round-trip journeys a day.

There are 1,665 stairs up to the top level, though tourists can only climb 720 of them, up as far as the second level. During a race in 1905, a gentleman climbed from the ground to the second floor—elevation gain 400 feet—in 3 minutes, 12 seconds.

First Level

(Note: A major renovation of the first level is scheduled for completion by fall 2014.)

The first level has more great views, all well-described by the tower's panorama displays. You can walk over a glass floor and look down to feel the rush of the sheer 200-foot vertical drop. The first level also has the majority of visitor services: WCs, a conference hall (closed to tourists), an ATM, and souvenirs. An upper-level area has multimedia displays (they change often) on the tower's construction, fireworks displays, virtual beam-walking, and place in pop culture. A small café sells pizza and sandwiches (outdoor tables in summer). The 58 Tour Eiffel restaurant has more *accessible* prices than the Jules Verne Restaurant above, and is also run by Alain Ducasse. In winter, part of the first level is sometimes set up for winter activities (most recently as an ice-skating rink).

In any weather, the tower stands strong. In the heat of summer, the sun warms the metal, causing the top to expand and lean about five inches away from the sun. Because of its lacy design, even the strongest of winds could never blow the tower down, only cause it to sway back and forth a few inches. In fact, Eiffel designed the tower primarily with wind resistance in mind, and many modern skyscrapers follow his mathematics.

Watch the original hydraulic pump (1889) at work. It once pumped water from this level to the second level to feed the machinery powering the upper elevator. Then look at the big wheels that wind and unwind heavy cables to lift the elevators.

▶ *Consider a drink or a sandwich while overlooking all of Paris, then take the elevator or stairs (5 minutes, 360 steps, free) to the ground.*

The Tour Ends

Welcome back to earth.

For a final look, stroll to Place du Trocadéro or to the end of the Champ de Mars and look back for great views of the tower. However impressive it may be by day, the tower is an awesome thing to see at twilight, when it becomes engorged with light, and virile Paris lies back and lets night be on top. When darkness fully envelops the city, the tower seems to climax with a spectacular light show at the top of each hour...for five minutes.

The tower is lit from within. At the top of the hour, it sparkles and projects a beacon of light.

Rue Cler Walk

The Art of Parisian Living

Paris is changing quickly, but a stroll down this open-air-market street introduces you to a thriving, traditional Parisian neighborhood and its local culture. Though somewhat upscale, Rue Cler retains the workaday charm of village Paris.

In food-crazy Paris, shopping for groceries is an integral part of everyday life. Rue Cler, traffic-free since 1984, is lined with the essential shops—wine, cheese, bread, chocolate—as well as a bank, a post office, and pleasant cafés.

To learn the fine art of living Parisian-style, there's no better classroom than Rue Cler. And you can assemble the ultimate French picnic. The Rue Cler Walk is the only tour in this guidebook you should start while hungry.

THE WALK BEGINS

▶ *Start your walk at the northern end of the pedestrian section of Rue Cler, at Rue de Grenelle (right by a bus #69 stop or a short walk from Mo: Ecole Militaire). Visit Rue Cler when its markets are open and lively (Tue-Sat 8:30-13:00 or 15:00-19:30, Sun 8:30-12:00, dead on Mon). Allow an hour to browse and café-hop along this short, three-block walk.*

❶ Café Roussillon

This neighborhood fixture recently dumped its old-fashioned, characteristic look for the latest café style—warm, natural wood tones, easy lighting, and music. To the right of the door, you'll see the *Tarif des Consommations* sign required by French law, making the pricing clear: Drinks served at the bar *(comptoir)* are cheaper than drinks served at the tables *(salles)*. Inside, the bar is always busy. The blackboard lists wines sold by the little 7-centiliter glass (about 2.5 ounces), along with other drinks.

The little **late-night grocery** next door is one of countless corner shops nicknamed *dépanneurs* ("to help you out of difficulty"). Open nightly until midnight, these stores are often run by hardworking North Africans willing to keep long hours. Locals happily pay the higher prices for the convenience *dépanneurs* provide.

▶ *If you're shopping for designer baby clothes, you'll find them across the street at...*

❷ Petit Bateau

The French spend at least as much on their babies as they do on their dogs—dolling them up with designer jammies. This store is one in a popular chain. Babies-in-the-know just aren't comfortable unless they're making a fashion statement (such as underwear with sailor stripes). Whereas much of Europe faces an aging and shrinking population, France is having a baby boom—an average of two children per family, compared to 1.6 for the rest of Europe. Babies are trendy, and the government rewards parents with substantial tax deductions for their first two children—and then doubles the deductions after that.

▶ *Cross Rue de Grenelle to find...*

❸ Top Halles Fruits and Vegetables

Each morning, fresh produce is trucked in from farmers' fields to Paris'

To Seine River

CAFE ROUSSILLON

PETIT BATEAU 2

■ "LATE-NIGHT" GROCERY

1

To Bus #69 stop & Eiffel Tower

RUE DE GRENELLE

TOP HALLES GREENGROCER 3

■ FRANPRIX

LE PETIT CLER CAFE 4

To Bus #69 stop & Army & Rodin Museums

TRAITEUR ASIATIQUE ■

■ GRAND HOTEL LEVEQUE

WINE BACCHUS 5

POISSONNERIE 7

FROMAGERIE 6

HORSE MEAT SIGN 8

RUE CLER

FLEURS ■

PHARMACY 9

CHARCUTERIE DAVOLI ■

OLDEST BUILDING & CHARCUTERIE-TRAITEUR JEUSSELIN 10

RUE VALADON

■ CHOCOLATS

FROMAGERIE ■

■ WINE NICOLAS

RUE DUVIVIER

CAFE DU MARCHE

LEADER PRICE BULK SHOPPING

L'EPICERIE FINE 12 11

■ LOANER BIKES

RUE DU CHAMP DE MARS

To Eiffel Tower

REAL ESTATE AGENCY

ARTISAN BOULANGERIE 13

RUE ERNEST PSICHARI

"A LA MERE DE FAMILLE" CONFECTIONERY 14

15 MEPHISTO SHOE STORE

CLER FLEURS 16

RUE BOSQUET

RUE CLER

BUTCHER ■

PASSAGE DE LA VIERGE

To Army & Rodin Museums

CITY INFO POST

PTT (POST) 17

To Ⓜ Ecole Militaire & Eiffel Tower

TABAC "LA CAVE A CIGARES" 18

AVENUE DE LA MOTTE PICQUET

25 Meters

25 Yards

Ⓜ

huge Rungis market—Europe's largest, near Orly Airport—and then dispatched to merchants with FedEx-like speed and precision. Good luck finding a shopping bag—locals bring their own two-wheeled carts or reusable bags. Also, notice how the earth-friendly French resist excessive packaging.

Parisians shop with their noses and buy foods in season. Try it. Sniff the odorless foreign strawberries (which locals call "plastic strawberries"), and compare with the odiferous torpedo-shaped French ones *(garriguettes)*. Explore. Find the herbs in the back—is today's delivery in? Check the melons and their country of origin—it must be posted. If they're from Guadeloupe, they're out of season, and many locals won't buy them.

The **Franprix** across the street is a small outpost of a nationwide supermarket chain. Opposite Grand Hôtel Lévêque is **Traiteur Asiatique.** Fast Asian food to go—about as common as bakeries now—has had an impact on traditional Parisian eating habits.

▶ Check out ➍ *Le Petit Cler, a trendy café that illustrates how this*

French Etiquette

As you enter a shop, always greet the store owner with *"Bonjour, Madame (or Monsieur)."* If you really want to win a clerk over, follow up your greeting with *"Excusez-moi de vous déranger"* (ek-skew-zay-mwah duh voo day-rahn-zhay)—Pardon me for bothering you—then ask for what you need. Remember that shopkeepers are busy serving regular customers, so don't get in the way. As you leave, complete the social interaction with *"Au revoir, Madame* (or *Monsieur)."*

On your walk, you'll likely see Parisian friends greeting each other with "Le French Kiss" *(faire la bise)*. This cheek-pecking is preferred to the American-style hug. Observe. They touch cheeks, pucker their lips, and make a gentle smacking sound—but the lips don't actually touch the cheek. Parisians *faire la bise* with two kisses—first right, then left—but some French people add more kisses. If it happens to you, my recommendation is to go for two with confidence, and then—hover and wait.

once-working-class market street is becoming increasingly upscale. Continue to...

❺ Wine Bacchus

After they've assembled their meal at other stores, shoppers come here to pick the appropriate wine. The clerk is a counselor who works with your needs and budget, and he can put a bottle of white in the fridge for you to pick up later. The wine is classified by region. Most "Parisians" (who are generally from elsewhere) have an affinity for the wines of their home region. You can get a fine bottle (especially the wines of the month in the center) for €12 (open until 20:00 except Sun).

▶ *Next door, smell the...*

❻ Fromagerie

Spilling outside into the street, this cheese shop offers more than 200 types of French cheese, both cow *(vache)* and goat *(chèvre)* cheese. The

A cheese for every day of the year

Parisians often shop daily.

place is lab-coat-serious but friendly. Known as a "BOF," it's where people buy *beurre, oeuf,* and *fromage*—butter, eggs, and cheese.

Notice the many cheese shapes—wedges, cylinders, balls, and miniature hockey pucks, all powdered white, gray, and burnt marshmallow. It's a festival of mold. The shape tells the buyer where the cheese is from—e.g., a pyramid is from the Loire region. This information is crucial. The region creates the *terroir*—the magical union of sun, soil, and farmer love—that gives the cheese its personality. *Ooh la la* means you're impressed. More *la*s means you're more impressed. *Ooh la la la la.* A Parisian friend once held the stinkiest glob close to her nose, took an orgasmic breath, and exhaled, "Yes, it smells like zee feet of angels."

In the back room, they store *les meules,* the big, 170-pound wheels of cheese, made from 250 gallons of milk. Although you don't eat the skin of these "hard" cheeses, the skin on most smaller cheeses—the Brie, the Camembert—is part of the taste. "It completes the package," says my local friend.

At dinner tonight you can take the cheese course just before or instead of dessert. On a good cheese plate you have a hard cheese (like Emmentaler—a.k.a. "Swiss cheese"), a flowery cheese (maybe Brie or Camembert), a bleu cheese, and a goat cheese—ideally from different regions. Because it's strongest, the goat cheese is usually eaten last.

▶ *Across the street, find the fish shop, known as the...*

❼ Poissonnerie

Fresh fish is brought into Paris daily from ports on the English Channel, 110 miles away. In fact, fish here is likely fresher than in many towns closer to the sea—anything still wiggling? This *poissonnerie,* like all such shops, was recently upgraded to meet the new Europe-wide hygiene standards.

▶ *Next door, check out the doorway (under the awning) at Crêperie Ulysée en Gaule.*

❽ No More Horse Meat

The stones and glass set over the doorway advertise horse meat: *Boucherie Chevaline.* While today this store serves souvlaki and crêpes, the classy 1930s storefront survives from the previous occupant. Signed by the artist, it's a work of art fit for a museum—but it belongs right here.

The door is decorated with lunch coupon decals (like *chèque déjeuner*) for local workers. In France, an employee lunch-subsidy program is an expected perk. Employers get a tax break for issuing voucher checks (worth about €8 each) for each day an employee works in a month. Sack lunches are rare, since a good lunch is sacred.

▶ *A few steps farther along is a flower shop. When visiting friends, French people give a gift of flowers. It's classiest to have them delivered before you show up. Across the street is the ❾ **Pharmacy.** In France, mildly sick people go first to the pharmacist, who has authority to diagnose and prescribe remedies.*

❿ Oldest Building and Charcuterie-Traiteur Jeucoolin

Next to the pharmacy is Rue Cler's oldest building (with the two garret windows on the roof). It's from the early 1800s, when this street was part of a village near Paris, and was lined with structures like this.

Now the house is a charcuterie-*traiteur*—a gourmet deli selling mouthwatering food to go. Because Parisian kitchens are so small, many Parisians—even great cooks—rely on these places for beautifully prepared side dishes to complement their home-cooked main course.

The charcuterie business is fiercely competitive. Jeusselin proudly displays its hard-won cooking-contest awards by the entrance. One reads: *Medaille d'Or du Fromage de Tête du Jambon blanc 2009*—gold medal for head cheese with white ham. Head cheese is a meat jelly made from the head of a pig or cow. Who would brag about that?? The French.

The other award—*Meilleur Traiteur de Paris, Gault & Millau 2008*—is for "best deli," determined by a prestigious food-rating organization. The prominently posted *Diplôme de Cordon Bleu* is a diploma from the most famous cooking school in France, which used to be in the neighborhood.

Even with such credentials, to stay competitive many charcuteries have added *traiteur* services: restaurant-style cooked dishes and tables for eating in. Jeusselin and its rival **Davoli** (across the street) go *mano a mano,* cooking up *plats du jour* (specials of the day), advertised on boards outside and inside.

To get the freshest food (e.g., a freshly roasted chicken on a spit), come just before lunch and dinner—around 11:00 or 17:00, when Parisians go grazing. Note the system: Order, take your ticket to the cashier to pay, and return with the receipt to pick up your food.

▶ *A few doors down is...*

⓫ Café du Marché

Café du Marché, on the corner, is *the* place to sit and enjoy the action (✪ see page 188). It's Rue Cler's living room, where locals gather before heading home, many staying for a relaxed and affordable dinner. The owner priced his menu so that locals could afford to dine out on a regular basis, and it worked—many patrons eat here five days a week. For a reasonable meal, grab a chair and check the chalk menu listing the *plat du jour.* Notice how the no-smoking-indoors laws have made outdoor seating and propane heaters a huge hit.

The shiny, sterile **Leader Price grocery store** (across the street) is a Parisian Costco, selling bulk items. But because storage space is so limited in Parisian apartments, few locals shop here. They buy their nonperishables online, their produce three times a week on Rue Cler, and their bread daily. The ugly exterior of this store suggests a sneaky bending of Rue Cler's normally rigorous design review for building permits.

▶ *Turn right and side-trip a couple doors down Rue du Champ de Mars to...*

⓬ L'Epicerie Fine

This fine-foods boutique stands out from the rest because of its gentle owners, Pascal and Nathalie. Their mission in life is to explain to travelers, in fluent English, what the French fuss over food is all about. Say *bonjour* and let them help you assemble a picnic. They'll tempt you with fine gourmet treats, Berthillon ice cream, and generous tastes of caramel, balsamic vinegar, and French and Italian olive oil (Tue-Fri 9:30-13:00 & 15:00-19:30, Sat-Sun 10:00-13:00, closed Mon, tel. 01 47 05 98 18).

▶ *Return to Rue Cler. The neighborhood bakery on the corner is often marked by a line of people waiting to pick up their daily baguette.*

⑬ Artisan Boulangerie

Since the French Revolution, the government has regulated the cost of a basic baguette. And to call your shop a *boulangerie,* by law you must do the baking on the premises. Locals debate the merits of Paris' many *boulangeries.* Some like their baguette a tad well-done while others prefer it more doughy. It's said that a baker cannot be both good at bread and good at pastry—at cooking school they major in one or the other. So a baker either bakes bread or makes pastries and has the other done elsewhere. But here, the baker does both, and nobody's complaining.

▶ *A bit farther along is...*

⑭ La Mère de Famille Gourmand Chocolats Confiseries

This shop has been in the neighborhood for 30 years. The wholesalers try to pressure the owner to push newer candies, but the owner has kept the old traditional ones, too. "The old ladies, they want the same sweets that made them so happy 80 years ago," she says. You can buy "naked bonbons" right out of the jar and chocolate by the piece (about €0.75 each). You're welcome to assemble a small assortment.

Until a few years ago, the chocolate was dipped and decorated right on the premises. As was the tradition in Rue Cler shops, the merchants resided and produced in the back and sold in the front.

▶ *Next door is a popular French-owned chain store,* ⑮ **Mephisto Shoes.** *In a city where many people don't own a car, good shoes matter. The average Parisian walks to the Métro, to work, to shop, and up the stairs to their apartment. Few Parisians join gyms. Across the street you'll find...*

⑯ Cler Fleurs

Almost all Parisians who reside in the city center—even the wealthiest—live in apartments or condos, with no yard. So Parisians spend small fortunes bringing nature into their homes with plants and fresh flower arrangements. Notice the flower boxes on balconies—you work with what you have.

The **butcher shop** a few doors down shows how far Parisians venture from beef when it comes to meat. You'll find rabbit, lamb, duck, veal, pigeon, pig's ears, liver, brain, and tripe—very photogenic.

▶ *Walk on to the end of Rue Cler, where it hits busy Avenue de la Motte-Picquet.*

⑰ City Info Post

This electronic signpost directs residents to websites for local information—transportation changes, surveys, employment opportunities, community events, and so on. Also nearby are big recycling stations—Paris is very "green." And why are all the trash cans made of see-through garbage sacks? Well, in the 1990s, there was a rash of nasty incidents where bad guys put rigged-up camp stove canisters into metal garbage cans, which exploded into deadly "shrapnel." With clear plastic bags, that won't happen again.

▶ *Across the busy street is a* tabac.

⑱ Tabac La Cave à Cigares

Just as the US has liquor stores licensed to sell booze, the only place for people over 16 to buy tobacco legally in France is at a *tabac* (tah-bah) counter. Notice how European laws require a bold warning sign on cigarettes—about half the size of the package—that says, bluntly, *fumer tue:* smoking kills.

A *tabac* sells more than just tobacco, and is a much-appreciated fixture of Parisian neighborhoods. It's a kind of government cash desk, selling stamps, public-transit tickets, and the always-popular LOTO tickets. Locals pay for parking meters by buying a card...or pay their fines here if they don't.

American smokers may not be able to resist the temptation to pick up a *petit Corona*—your chance to buy a fine Cuban cigar without breaking US law.

▶ *The Ecole Militaire Métro stop is just down Avenue de la Motte-Picquet to the right. If you bought a picnic along this walk, here are two good places to enjoy it: Leaving Rue Cler, turn left on Avenue de la Motte-Picquet for the Army Museum (find the small park after crossing Boulevard de la Tour-Maubourg). Or, turn right to reach the Champs de Mars park (and the Eiffel Tower).*

Versailles

Château de Versailles

If you've ever wondered why your American passport has French writing in it, you'll find the answer at Versailles (vehr-"sigh")—every king's dream palace. The powerful court of Louis XIV at Versailles set the standard of culture for all of Europe, right up to modern times.

Versailles has three blockbuster sights. The palace itsel—the Château—features the lavish, chandeliered living rooms of France's kings. The expansive Gardens are a landscaped wonderland of statues and fountains. Finally, the Trianon Palaces and Domaine de Marie-Antoinette offer a pastoral getaway of small palaces, including Marie's faux-peasant Hamlet.

Versailles is big and crowded, so arm yourself with a pass to skip ticket-buying lines. Arrive early or late to avoid crowds.

ORIENTATION

Cost: I recommend buying either a Paris Museum Pass or Versailles' combo-ticket called "Le Passeport," both of which cover your entrance to the most important parts of the complex. If you don't get a pass, you can buy individual tickets for each of the three different sections:

• **The Château,** the main palace, costs €15 (free on first Sun Nov-March).

• **The Trianon Palaces and Domaine de Marie-Antoinette**— the small palaces in the far corner of the Gardens—cost €10 (free on first Sun Nov-March).

• **The Gardens** are free, except on Fountain Spectacle days, when admission is €8.50 (weekends April-Oct plus many Tue).

The Le Passeport one-day combo-ticket covers all three sections. It costs €18, or €25 on Fountain Spectacle days. The handy Paris Museum Pass covers the Château and the Trianon/Domaine area (a €25 value), but you'll have to buy an additional ticket for any Fountain Spectacles.

Hours: The **Château** is open April-Oct Tue-Sun 9:00-18:30, Nov-March Tue-Sun 9:00-17:30, closed Mon year-round.

The **Trianon Palaces and Domaine de Marie-Antoinette** are open April-Oct Tue-Sun 12:00-18:30, Nov-March Tue-Sun 12:00-17:30, closed Mon year-round (off-season only the two Trianon Palaces are open, not the Hamlet or other outlying buildings).

The **Gardens** are open April-Oct daily 9:00-20:30; Nov-March Tue-Sun 8:00-18:00, closed Mon.

Last entry to all of these areas is 30 minutes before closing.

Crowd-Beating Strategies: Versailles is a zoo May-Sept 10:00-13:00, with especially big crowds all day Tue and Sun. Any day the fountains play, the whole complex can be unbearably crowded dawn to dusk. Lines to buy tickets and go through security are long, and the Château is a slow shuffle of shoulder-to-shoulder tourists. To minimize these crowds, arrive by 9:00 or come after 14:00, and avoid Tue, Sun, and fountain days. If you can't arrive before the midmorning crowds set in, consider touring the Gardens first, then visit the Château after 14:00 when crowds (somewhat) dissipate.

To avoid the long lines at the Château box office (to the left as you face the palace), buy tickets and passes in advance at the

Versailles city TI (see "Information," below). They're also available at any Paris TI or FNAC department store, or online at chateauversailles. fr (print out your pass/ticket or pick it up near the entrance). If you do wait to buy tickets at the Château, walk straight to the back of the box office to use the ticket machines (requires cash or chip-and-PIN card). You can also avoid ticket-buying lines by booking a guided tour (see below). Note that even advance ticket and pass holders must wait in line to go through security (longest lines 10:00-12:00).

Here's how I'd spend the day at Versailles: Leave Paris by 8:00 to beat the crowds. Tour the Château, then break for lunch in the Gardens. Spend the afternoon touring the Gardens and the Trianon/ Domaine. Have dinner in Versailles town, then head back to Paris.

Pickpockets: Assume pickpockets are working the tourist crowds.

Getting There: The town of Versailles is 30 minutes southwest of Paris. Take the RER-C train (4/hour, 30-40 minutes one-way, €6.50 round-trip) from any of these Paris RER stops: Gare d'Austerlitz, St. Michel, Musée d'Orsay, Invalides, Pont de l'Alma, and Champ de Mars. Scan the list of departing trains. Any train whose name starts with a V (e.g., "Vick") goes to Versailles; don't board other trains. Get off at the last stop (Versailles Château R.G., or "Rive Gauche"). Exit through the turnstiles by inserting your ticket. To reach the palace, turn right out of the train station, then left at the first boulevard, and walk 10 minutes. To return to Paris, all trains serve all downtown Paris RER stops on the C line. Taxis for the 30-minute ride (without traffic) cost about €60.

Information: Tel. 01 30 83 78 00. The excellent website has the latest changes and calendar of special events—chateauversailles.fr. The uncrowded and helpful Versailles city TI (daily 9:00-19:00, tel. 01 39 24 88 88) is in town on your walk from the RER station to the palace—it's just past the Pullman Hôtel. The Château's information office (long lines) is on the left side of the courtyard as you face the Château (toll tel. 08 10 81 16 14).

Guided Tours: Ninety-minute English tours of the Château often sell out; book online or immediately upon arrival at the guided-tours office in the Château courtyard, just to the right as you approach the palace (€16 includes palace entry, €7 if you have a pass).

Audioguides: A free audioguide to the Château is included in admission. Other podcasts and digital tours are available in the "multimedia"

Versailles

Versailles

Petit Canal

Grand Canal

TRIANON PALACES & DOMAINE DE MARIE-ANTOINETTE

EXIT

GRAND TRIANON

FRENCH PAVILION

B To **T** Train Stn.

THEATER   BELVEDERE

WC

WALL

THE HAMLET

TOWER

PETIT TRIANON

TEMPLE OF LOVE

See detail map

T

ALLEE DE LA REINE

ALLEE DES MATELOTS

BOAT RENTAL   **T**

RESTAURANT & SNACKS

ALLEE ST. ANTOINE

BIKE & GOLF CART RENTAL

ALLEE D'APOLLON

Apollo Basin

WC

AVE. DE TRIANON

KING'S GARDEN

GARDENS

COLONNADE

OBELISK GROVE

ROYAL DRIVE

STAR GROVE

MIRROR FOUNTAIN

WC & SNACK KIOSK

Latona Basin

WC

APOLLO'S BATHS GROVE

QUEEN'S GROVE

BIKE RENTAL

PORTE DE LA REINE

WALKING TIMES
Train Station to Château = 10 min
Château to Grand Trianon = 30 min
Grand Trianon to the Hamlet = 15 min
Trianon/Domaine-Place du Marché = 40 min

T Petit Train Stop

B Phebus Shuttle Bus

200 Meters
200 Yards

T

B

Neptune Basin

ORANGERIE

GOLF-CART RENTAL

TICKET SALES

See detail map

CHATEAU

GUIDED TOURS

BOULEVARD DU ROI

Place d'Armes

Place Hoche

RUE CARNOT

RUE DE LA PAROISSE

BOULEVARD DE LA REINE

STABLES

STABLES

AVE. DE SCEAUX

AVENUE DE PARIS

AVE. DE ST-CLOUD

NOTRE DAME

TOWN

AVE. DE L'EUROPE

RUE DU MARECHAL FOCH

B

To Paris

RER TRAIN STATION (RIVE GAUCHE)

Place du Marché

RIVE DROITE TRAIN STATION

To Paris (St. Lazare Station)

section at chateauversailles.fr. Or you can download a free Rick Steves audio tour (✪ see page 207).

Length of This Day Trip: With the usual lines, allow 1.5 hours each for the Château, the Gardens, and the Trianon/Domaine. Add another two hours for round-trip transit, plus another hour for lunch...and, at around eight hours, Versailles is a full day trip from Paris.

Baggage Check: To enter the Château and the two Trianons, you must use the free baggage check for large bags and baby strollers.

Services: Reminiscent of the days when dukes urinated behind the potted palm trees, WCs at the Château are few and far between. The most reliable WCs are immediately upon entering the Château (Entrance H) and near the Grand Café d'Orléans. In the Gardens, lesser WCs are near the Latona Basin, at the Grand Canal, in the Grand Trianon and Petit Trianon, and several others.

Eating: The Grand Café d'Orléans, to the left of the Château's entrance, offers good-value self-service meals (€5 sandwiches, great for picnicking in the Gardens). In the Gardens, you'll find several restaurants, cafés, and snack stands. Most are clustered near the Latona Fountain (less crowded) and the Grand Canal (more crowds and more choices, including two restaurants).

In the town (east of the Château), several colorful eateries line lively Place du Marché Notre-Dame, including crêpes at Á la Côte Bretonne. Handy McDonald's and Starbucks (both with WCs) are near the train station.

Photography: Allowed, but no flash indoors.

Fountain Spectacles: On certain days in spring and summer, piped-in classical music accompanies impressive fountain displays. The fountains run April-Oct Sat-Sun 11:00-12:00 & 15:30-17:30 (finale at Neptune Fountain at 17:20). They also run on Tue late May-late June at 11:00-12:00 & 14:30-16:00. On these spray days, the Gardens cost €8.50. On other Tue April-Oct you get all-day music, but no water (€7.50). Elaborate sound-and-light displays are staged on Sat nights (and some Fri) mid-June-mid-Sept at 21:00 (€23). The schedule changes, so see the full calendar at chateauversailles.fr.

Starring: Luxurious palaces, endless gardens, Louis XIV, Marie-Antoinette, and the *ancien régime.*

THE TOUR BEGINS

▶ *Stand in the huge courtyard and face the palace, or Château. The ticket-buying office is to the left. The entrance to the Château (once you have your ticket or pass) is through the modern concrete-and-glass security checkpoint, marked Entrance A.*

On this self-guided tour, we'll see the Château, the landscaped Gardens in the "backyard," and the Trianon Palaces and Domaine de Marie-Antoinette, located at the far end of the Gardens.

Exterior—The Original Château and the Courtyard

The section of the palace with the clock is the original château, once a small hunting lodge where little Louis XIV spent his happiest boyhood years. Naturally, the Sun King's private bedroom (the three arched windows beneath the clock) faced the rising sun. The palace and grounds are laid out on an east–west axis.

Once king, Louis XIV expanded the lodge by attaching wings, creating the present U-shape. Later, the long north and south wings were built. The total cost of the project has been estimated at half of France's entire GNP for one year.

Think how busy this courtyard must have been 300 years ago. As many as 5,000 nobles were here at any one time, each with an entourage. They'd buzz from games to parties to amorous rendezvous in sedan-chair taxis. Servants ran about delivering secret messages and roast legs of lamb. Horse-drawn carriages arrived at the fancy gate with their finely dressed passengers, having driven up the broad boulevard that

Entrance A—security checkpoint

Original Château and courtyard

We Three Kings

Versailles was the residence of the king and the seat of France's government for a hundred years. With 18 million people united under one king (England had only 5.5 million), a booming economy, and a powerful military, France was Europe's number-one power. Versailles was the cultural heartbeat of Europe. Everyone learned French. French taste in clothes, hairstyles, table manners, theater, music, art, and kissing spread across the Continent.

Three kings lived in Versailles during its century of glory:

Louis XIV (reigned 1643-1715), Europe's greatest king, built Versailles and established French dominance.

Louis XV (r. 1715-1774) was his great-grandson. (Louis XIV had reigned for 72 years, outliving several heirs.) Louis XV carried on the tradition and policies, but without the Sun King's flair. France's power abroad was weakening, and there were rumblings of rebellion from within.

Louis XVI (r. 1774-1792)—a shy, meek bookworm—inherited a nation in crisis. He married a sweet girl from the Austrian royal family, Marie-Antoinette, and together they retreated into the idyllic gardens of Versailles while Revolutionary fires smoldered.

ran directly from Paris. Then, as now, there were hordes of tourists, pickpockets, palace workers, and men selling wind-up children's toys.

▶ *After passing through security at Entrance A, you spill out into the open-air courtyard inside the golden Royal Gate. Enter the Château at Entrance H—the State Apartments. Once inside, there's an info desk (get a free map), WCs, and free audioguides. Glance through a doorway at the impressive Royal Chapel, which we'll see again upstairs.*

Just follow the flow of crowds through a number of rooms (the route and exhibits change frequently). Climb the stairs and pass through more exhibits. Finally, you reach a palatial golden-brown room, with a doorway that overlooks the Royal Chapel.

Royal Chapel

Dut-dutta-dah! Every morning at 10:00, the musicians struck up the music, these big golden doors opened, and Louis XIV and his family stepped onto the balcony to attend Mass. While Louis looked down on the golden altar, the lowly nobles on the ground floor knelt with their backs to the altar and looked up—worshipping Louis worshipping God. Important religious ceremonies took place here, including the marriage of young Louis XVI to Marie-Antoinette.

In the vast pagan "temple" that is Versailles—built to glorify one man, Louis XIV—this Royal Chapel is a paltry tip of the hat to that "other" god... the Christian one.

▶ *Enter the next room, an even more sumptuous space with a fireplace and a colorful painting on the ceiling.*

The Royal Chapel, where Louis VIX worshipped and allowed himself to be worshipped.

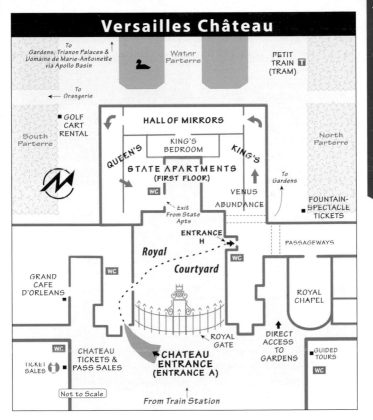

Hercules Drawing Room

Pleasure ruled. The main suppers, balls, and receptions were held in this room. Picture elegant partygoers in fine silks, wigs, rouge, lipstick, and fake moles (and that's just the men), as they dance to the strains of a string quartet.

On the wall opposite the fireplace is an appropriate painting showing Christ in the middle of a Venetian party. The work by Paolo Veronese was one of Louis XIV's favorites, so they decorated the room around it.

Louis XIV—The Sun King

Louis XIV was a true Renaissance man, a century after the
Renaissance: athletic, good-
looking, a musician, dancer,
horseman, statesman, art-lover,
lover. He was a good listener
who could put even commoners
at ease.

Louis XIV, age 63, by Hyacinthe Rigaud

Louis had grown up in the
previous royal residence—the
Louvre in Paris. When he
became king, he moved the
government to the forests of Versailles, where he'd hunted as a kid.
There, he could concentrate power around himself. He invited France's
nobles—who in other countries were the center of power—to live at
Versailles. They became virtual slaves of pleasure, dependent on Louis'
generosity, while he made the important decisions.

Louis called himself the Sun King because he gave life and warmth
to all he touched. He was also thought of as Apollo, the Greek god of
the sun. Versailles became the personal temple of this god on earth,
decorated with statues and symbols of Apollo, the sun, and Louis XIV
himself.

For 70 years he was the perfect embodiment of the absolute mon-
arch. He summed it up best himself with his famous rhyme—"*L'état,
c'est moi!*" (lay-tah say-mwah): "The state, that's me!"

Stand by the fireplace for the full effect: The room's columns, arches, and
frieze match the height and style of Veronese's painted architecture, which
makes the painting an extension of the room.

The ceiling painting creates the effect of a sunroof opening up to
heaven. Hercules (with his club) hurries up to heaven on a chariot, late
for his wedding to the king of the gods' daughter. The scene echoes real
life—Louis XIV built the room for his own daughter's wedding reception.

▶ *From here on it's a one-way tour—getting lost is not allowed. Follow the* crowds into the small green room with a ceiling painting showing a goddess in pink showering riches on invited guests. The names of the rooms generally come from the paintings on the ceilings.

Salon of Abundance

If the party in the Hercules Room got too intense, you could always step in here for some refreshments. Silver trays were loaded up with liqueurs, exotic stimulants (coffee), juice, chocolates, and, on really special occasions, Doritos and guacamole.

Louis XIV was a gracious host who enjoyed letting his hair down at night. If he took a liking to you, he might sneak you through those doors there (in the middle of the wall) and into his own private study, where he'd show off his collection of dishes, medals, jewels, or...the *Mona Lisa,* which hung on his wall.

Venus Room

Love ruled at Versailles. In this room, couples would cavort beneath the goddess of love, floating on the ceiling. Venus sends down a canopy of golden garlands to ensnare mortals in delicious *amour*. Notice how a painted garland goes "out" the bottom of the central painting, becomes a golden garland held by a satyr, transforms into a gilded wood garland, and then turns back into a painting again. Baroque artists loved to mix their media to fool the eye.

Don't let the statue of a confident Louis XIV as a Roman emperor fool you. He started out as a poor little rich kid with a chip on his shoulder. The French *parlements* treated little Louis and his mother as virtual prisoners in their home, the Royal Palace in Paris (today's Louvre). There they eked by

Hercules among the gods   Venus Room ceiling painting

Versailles

with bland meals, hand-me-down leotards, and pointed shoes. After Louis XIV attained power, he made Versailles a pleasure palace—his way of saying that "Living well is the best revenge."

Diana Room

Here in the billiards room, Louis and his men played on a table that stood in the center of the room, while ladies sat surrounding them on Persian-carpet cushions, and music wafted in from next door. Louis was a good pool player, a sore loser, and a king—thus, he rarely lost.

The famous bust of Louis by Giovanni Lorenzo Bernini (in the center) shows a handsome, dashing, 27-year-old playboy-king. His gaze is steady amid his windblown cloak and hair. Young Louis loved life. He hunted animals by day (notice Diana the Huntress, with her bow, on the ceiling) and chased beautiful women at night.

Games were actually an important part of Louis' political strategy, known as "the domestication of the nobility." By distracting the nobles with the pleasures of courtly life, he was free to run the government his way. Gambling was popular (especially a blackjack-type card game), and Louis lent money to the losers, making them even more indebted to him. The good life was an addiction, and Louis kept the medicine cabinet well-stocked.

As you move into the next room, notice the fat walls that hid thin servants, who were to be at their master's constant call—but out of sight when not needed.

Mars Room

This red room, home to Louis' Swiss bodyguards, has a military flair. On the

Venus Room—Louis XIV as emperor

Mercury Room—the king's official bedroom

ceiling there's Mars, the Greek god of war, in a chariot pulled by wolves. As you wander, remember that the carpets, mirrors, furniture, and tapestries we see today are (generally) not original, but are from the same period.

Mercury Room

Louis' life was a work of art. Everything he did was a public event designed to show his subjects how it should be done. This room may have served as Louis' official (not actual) bedroom, where the Sun King would ritually rise each morning to warm his subjects.

From a canopied bed (like this 18th-century one), Louis would get up, dress, and take a seat for morning prayer. Meanwhile, the nobles would stand behind a balustrade, in awe of his piety, nobility, and clean socks. At breakfast they murmured with delight as he deftly decapitated his boiled egg with a knife. And when Louis went to bed at night, the dukes and barons would fight over who got to hold the candle while he slipped into his royal jammies.

Apollo Room

This was the grand throne room. Louis held court from a 10-foot-tall, silver-and-gold, canopied throne on a raised platform placed in the center of the room.

Everything in here reminds us of Louis XIV's glory. On the ceiling the sun god Apollo (representing Louis) drives his chariot, dragging the sun across the heavens to warm the four corners of the world—including good ol' America, symbolized by an Indian maiden with a crocodile.

The famous portrait by Hyacinthe Rigaud over the fireplace gives a more human look at Louis XIV, age 63. He's shown in a dancer's pose, displaying the legs that made him one of the all-time dancing fools of kingery. At night they often held parties in this room, actually dancing around the throne. Louis had more than 300 wigs like this one. The fashion sprouted all over Europe, even spreading to the American colonies.

Louis XIV may have been treated like a god, but his subjects adored him as a symbol of everything a man could be, the fullest expression of the Renaissance Man.

▶ *Continue into the final room of the King's Wing.*

The War Room

"Louis Quatorze was addicted to wars," and the room depicts his victories over the rest of Europe—in marble, gilding, stucco, and paint. On the ceiling, Lady France hurls down thunderbolts at her enemies. The stucco relief on the wall shows Louis XIV on horseback, triumphing over his fallen enemies. But Louis' greatest triumph may be the next room, the one that everybody wrote home about.

The Hall of Mirrors

No one had ever seen anything like this hall when it was opened. Mirrors were still a great luxury at the time, and the number and size of these monsters was astounding. The hall is nearly 250 feet long. There are 17 arched mirrors, matched by 17 windows letting in that breathtaking view of the Gardens. Lining the hall are 24 gilded candelabra, eight busts of Roman emperors, and eight classical-style statues (seven of them ancient). The ceiling shows Louis in the central panel doing what he did best—triumphing.

Imagine this place lit by the flames of thousands of candles, filled with ambassadors, nobles, and guests dressed in silks and powdered wigs.

The Hall of Mirrors—a grand ballroom of chandeliers, mirrored walls, and staggering views

At the far end of the room sits the king, on the canopied throne moved in temporarily from the Apollo Room. Servants glide by with silver trays of hors d'oeuvres, and an orchestra fuels the festivities. The mirrors reflect an age when beautiful people loved to look at themselves. It was no longer a sin to be proud of good looks or to enjoy the good things in life: laughing, dancing, eating, drinking, flirting, and watching the sun set into the distant canal.

From the center of the hall you can fully appreciate the epic scale of Versailles. The huge palace (by architect Louis Le Vau), the fantasy interior (by Charles Le Brun), and the endless Gardens (by André Le Nôtre) made Versailles *le* best. In 1919, Germany and the Allies signed the Treaty of Versailles, ending World War I (and, some say, starting World War II) right here, in the Hall of Mirrors.

▶ *From the Hall of Mirrors, a short detour to the left takes you to the center of the palace...*

King's Bedroom and Council Rooms

Pass through a first large room to find Louis XIV's bedroom. With an impressive bed and balustrade, it's elaborately decorated. The decor changed with the season. Look out the window and notice how this small room is at the exact center of the immense horseshoe-shaped building, overlooking the main courtyard and—naturally—facing the rising sun in the east. It symbolized the exact center of power in France. Imagine the humiliation on that day in 1789 when Louis' great-great-great-grandson, Louis XVI, was forced to stand here and acknowledge the angry crowds that filled the square demanding the end of the divine monarchy.

▶ *Return to the Hall of Mirrors. At the far end is the...*

Peace Room

By the end of the Sun King's long life, he was tired of fighting. In this sequel to the War Room, peace is granted to Europe as cupids play with the discarded cannons, and swords are transformed into violins. Louis XIV advised his great-grandson—the future Louis XV—to "be a peaceful king." The oval painting above the fireplace shows 19-year-old Louis XV, with his wife and twins, bestowing an olive branch on Europe.

▶ *The Peace Room marks the beginning of the queen's half of the palace. Enter the first room of the Queen's Wing, with its canopied bed.*

King's Bedroom—heart of the palace

Napoleon—revolutionary with a crown

The Queen's Bedchamber

It was here that the queen rendezvoused with her husband. Two queens died here, and this is where 19 princes were born. Royal babies were delivered in public to prove their blue-bloodedness. (The large canopied bed is a reconstruction.)

True, Louis XIV was not the most faithful husband. The Sun King warmed more than one bed, for he was above the rules of mere mortals. Adultery became acceptable—even fashionable—in court circles. Some of Louis XIV's (and XV's) mistresses became more famous and powerful than their queens. But Louis XIV made a point of sleeping with the queen as often as possible—the secret-looking door on the left side of the bed led straight to his rooms.

This room looks just like it did in the days of the final queen, Marie-Antoinette, who substantially redecorated the entire wing. That's her bust over the fireplace, and the double eagle of her native Austria in the corners. The big mahogany chest to the left of the bed held her jewels.

Salon of the Nobles

Here, in this mint-green room, the wife of Louis XV and her circle of friends met, under paintings by Boucher—popular with the queen for their pink-cheeked Rococo exuberance. Discussions ranged from politics to gossip, food to literature, fashion to philosophy. All three of Versailles' rulers considered themselves enlightened monarchs who promoted the arts and new ideas. Louis XIV laughed at the anti-authoritarian plays of Molière, and Louis XV gave free room and board here to the political radical Voltaire. Ironically, these discussions planted the seeds of liberal thought that would grow into the Revolution.

Queen's Antechamber (Grand Couvert)

The royal family dined here publicly, while servants and nobles fluttered around them, admired their table manners, and laughed at the king's jokes like courtly Paul Shaffers. A typical dinner consisted of four different soups, two whole birds stuffed with truffles, mutton, ham slices, fruit, pastries, compotes, and preserves.

The central portrait is of luxury-loving, "let-them-eat-cake" Marie-Antoinette, who became a symbol of decadence to the peasants. The portrait at the far end is a public-relations attempt to soften her image by showing her with three of her children.

Queen's Guard Room

On October 5, 1789, a mob of Revolutionaries stormed the palace. They were fed up with the ruling class leading a life of luxury in the countryside while they were starving in the grimy streets of Paris.

King Louis XVI and his queen Marie-Antoinette locked themselves in. The Revolutionaries burst into this room where Marie-Antoinette was hiding, overcame her bodyguards, ransacked the palace, and dragged her off with her husband. (Some claim that, as they carried her away, she sang, "Louis, Louis, oh-oh...we gotta go now.") Eventually, the king and queen were brought to the Place de la Concorde in Paris, where they knelt under the guillotine and were made a foot shorter at the top.

Coronation Room

No sooner did the French throw out a king than they got an emperor. The Revolution established a shaky democracy, but it was usurped by the upstart general Napoleon Bonaparte, who soon conquered Europe. The huge canvas on the left-hand wall (a copy of the Louvre's version) captures Napoleon's "crowning" moment—making himself and his kneeling wife, Josephine, emperor and empress.

▸ *This ends our tour of the Château, but there is more—the History of France rooms (on this floor) and the modestly furnished Dauphin's and Mesdames Apartments (downstairs).*

When you're ready to exit, stairs lead from the Coronation Room down to the ground floor. Exit the palace and follow signs to the Gardens (les Jardins), *located behind the Château.*

Consider a lunch break before tackling the Gardens.

THE GARDENS

Louis XIV was a divine-right ruler. One way he proved it was by controlling nature like a god. These lavish grounds—elaborately planned, pruned, and decorated—showed everyone that Louis was in total command.

▶ *Entering the Gardens, go to the far left to reach the stone railing that overlooks...*

The Orangerie

The warmth from the Sun King was so great that he could even grow orange trees in chilly France. Louis XIV had a thousand of these to amaze his visitors. In winter they were kept in the greenhouses (beneath your feet) that surround the courtyard. On sunny days, they were wheeled out in their silver planters and scattered around the grounds.

▶ *Make an about-face and walk back toward the palace. Sit on the top stairs and look away from the palace.*

View Down the Royal Drive

This, to me, is the most stunning spot in all of Versailles. With the palace behind you, it seems as if the grounds stretch out forever. Versailles was laid out along an eight-mile axis that included the grounds, the palace, and the town of Versailles itself, one of the first instances of urban planning since Roman times and a model for future capitals, such as Washington, DC, and Brasilia.

Looking down the Royal Drive, you see the round Apollo fountain far in the distance. Just beyond that is the Grand Canal. The groves on either side of the Royal Drive were planted with trees from all over, laid out in an

The Orangerie—gardens and greenhouses

View down the Royal Drive—eight-mile axis

Getting Around the Gardens

On Foot: It's a 45-minute walk (plus sightseeing) from the palace, down to the Grand Canal, past the two Trianon palaces, to the Hamlet at the far end of Domaine de Marie-Antoinette.

By Bike: There's a bike rental station by the Grand Canal (€6.50/hour). You can't take your bike inside the grounds of the Trianon/Domaine, but you can park it outside an entrance.

By _Petit Train_: The fast-looking, slow-moving tram travels a one-way, 50-minute route: from the Château (north side) to the Grand and Petit Trianons, Grand Canal, and back to the Château (€7 RT, pay driver).

By Golf Cart: These are fun, but you can't take them inside the Trianon/Domaine and they only go along a prescribed route (€30/hour, steep late fees, rent at Château or Grand Canal).

elaborate grid, and dotted with statues and fountains. Of the original 1,500 fountains, 300 remain.

▸ *Stroll down the steps to get a good look at the frogs and lizards that fill the round...*

Latona Basin

Atop the fountain stands Apollo (the sun god) as a child, with his sister and mom, Latona. Latona, an unwed mother, was insulted by the local peasants, so Zeus swooped down and turned them into toads and newts.

▸ *As you continue down the Royal Drive, you'll pass by "ancient" statues done by 17th-century French sculptors. Our next stop—the Colonnade—is hidden in the woods on the left-hand side of the Royal Drive, about three-fourths of the way to the Apollo Basin.*

The Colonnade

Versailles had no prestigious ancient ruins, so the king built this prefab Roman ruin—a 100-foot circle of 64 marble columns supporting arches. Nobles could picnic in the shade, watching the birdbath fountains spout, listening to a string quartet, and pretending they were enlightened citizens of the ancient world.

The Apollo Basin

The fountains of Versailles were its most famous attraction, and this one—of the sun god—was the centerpiece. Apollo, in his sunny chariot, starts his journey across the sky. The horses are half-submerged, giving the impression, when the fountains play, of the sun rising out of the mists of dawn.

All of Versailles' fountains are gravity-powered. They work on the same principle as blocking a hose with your finger to make it squirt. Underground streams (pumped into Versailles by Seine River pressure) feed into smaller pipes at the fountains, which shoot the water high into the air.

Looking back at the palace from here, realize that the distance you just walked is only a fraction of this vast complex of buildings, gardens, and waterways. Be glad you don't have to mow the lawn.

The Grand Canal

In an era before virtual reality, this was the next best thing to an actual trip to Venice. Imported Venetian gondoliers would pole along the waters

The Apollo Basin—The sun god rises from the mist on days when the fountains play.

accompanied by barges with orchestras playing "O Sole Mio." The canal is one mile from end to end.

The Grand Canal hosts eateries, rental boats, bike and golf-cart rentals, and a *Petit Train* tram stop.

▶ *The area called the Trianon Palaces and Domaine de Marie-Antoinette is a 10-minute walk from the Grand Canal. There are three entrances to the walled enclosure: near the Grand Trianon palace (where we'll enter), near the Petit Trianon palace, or near the Hamlet.*

To get to the Grand Trianon, start walking up the Grand Canal (✪ see the map on page 143). About 70 yards past the boat rental (and immediately past the restaurant), veer right. You'll find twin dirt paths flanking a lo-o-ong strip of lawn. This leads uphill 500 yards to the Grand Trianon.

THE TRIANON PALACES AND DOMAINE DE MARIE-ANTOINETTE

Versailles began as an escape from the pressures of kingship. But in a short time, the Château had become as stressful as Paris ever was—sniping politics, strict etiquette, and 24/7 scrutiny. Louis XIV and his successors needed an escape from their escape. They built this fantasy world of palaces and pleasure gardens and retreated further and further from everyday life.

Grand Trianon

Delicate, pink, and set amid gardens, the Grand Trianon was the perfect summer getaway. Louis XIV built it for his mistress. They spent a couple of nights a week here, near the tiny peasant village of Trianon—hence the name.

Inside, the rooms are a complex overlay of furnishings from many different kings, dauphins, and nobles that have lived here over the centuries. Louis XIV alone had three different bedrooms. Concentrate on the illustrious time of Louis XIV (1688-1715) and Napoleon Bonaparte (1810-1814).

The spacious Mirror Room (Salon des Glaces, Room 3) has the original white walls and mirrors of Louis XIV, and the Empire-style furniture of Napoleon (unornamented, high-polished wood, with classical motifs). In Louis XIV's Bedchamber (Chambre de l'Impératrice, Room 4), imagine waking up in this big bed with your lover, throwing back the curtain, and

Louis XIV's bedroom—Wake up with the king.

Grand Trianon—gardens in back

looking out the windows at the gardens. Exit into the open-air colonnade (Peristyle) that connects the two wings and admire the gardens. The flowers were changed daily for the king's pleasure—for new color combinations and new "nasal cocktails."

▶ ✪ *Use the map on page 143 to explore the rest of the Trianon/Domaine grounds. You'll meander along pathways through woods and gardens that lead you naturally from sight to sight. Exiting the Grand Trianon, circle the building clockwise, then follow signs to the* Petit Trianon. *Your first stop is the...*

French Pavilion

This small, white building with rooms fanning out from the center has big French doors to let in a cool breeze. Here Marie-Antoinette spent summer evenings with family and friends, listening to music or playing parlor games, exploring all avenues of *la douceur de vivre*—the sweetness of living.

French Pavilion—one of many hidden gems

Belvedere—tiny palace above a pond

Domaine de Marie-Antoinette

▶ Up ahead is the cube-shaped Petit Trianon. But midway there, detour left to find...

Marie-Antoinette's Theater (Le Théâtre de la Reine)
Marie-Antoinette was an aspiring performer. In this plush, fully-functioning, 100-seat doll-house theater, she and her friends acted out plays for a select audience.

▶ Just before reaching the Petit Trianon, turn left and find the nearby...

Belvedere, Rock, and Grotto
A pond graced with a tiny palace flanked by a fake mountain—how bucolic. The octagonal Belvedere palace is as much windows as it is walls. When the doors were open, it could serve as a gazebo for musicians, serenading nobles in this man-made alpine setting. To the right of the Belvedere (you'll have to find it) is the secret Grotto.

▶ *Facing the Belvedere, turn right (east) and follow the pond's meandering stream. Continue frolicking along the paths till you spy a round, fanciful tower and a smattering of rustic, half-timbered buildings fronting a lake—the Hansel-and-Gretel-like hamlet.*

The Hamlet (Le Village du Hameau)

Marie-Antoinette longed for the simple life of a peasant—not the hard labor of real peasants, who sweated and starved around her, but the fairytale world of simple country pleasures.

This was an actual working farm with a dairy (by the tower), a water mill, a pigeon coop *(Le Colombier),* and a menagerie where her servants kept cows, goats, and chickens. The Queen's House—two buildings connected by a wooden skywalk—was like any typical peasant farmhouse, with a billiard room, library, dining hall, and two living rooms.

The Hamlet—a faux peasant village where Marie-Antoinette indulged her fantasies

Temple of Love—perfect for a rendezvous

Petit Trianon—four-faced palace

▶ *As you head back toward the Petit Trianon, you'll pass by the white dome of the...*

Temple of Love

A circle of 12 white marble Corinthian columns supports a dome, decorating a path where lovers could stroll. It's a delightful monument to a society where the rich could afford that ultimate luxury, romantic love.

Petit Trianon

Louis XV's first mistress, Madame de Pompadour, built the Petit Trianon ("Small Trianon"), and it later became home to his next mistress, Madame du Barry.

The gray, cubical building is a masterpiece of Neoclassical architecture. It has four distinct facades, each a perfect and harmonious combination of Greek-style columns, windows, and railings. You can tour the handsome interior. The Baroque WC was ahead of its time.

When Louis XVI became king, he gave the building to his new bride, Marie-Antoinette. She made it her home and installed a carousel on the lawn outside. Here she played, while in the cafés of faraway Paris, revolutionaries plotted the end of the *ancien régime*.

▶ *The real world and the main Château are a 30-minute walk to the southeast. If you've had enough walking, you can ride the* Petit Train *from here back to the Château. Or, to return directly to the Versailles Château R.G. train station, go 150 yards up the road to the Grand Trianon to catch the Phébus shuttle bus (runs hourly mid-April-Oct only, €2 or one Métro ticket).*

Sights

Paris is blessed with world-class museums and monuments—more than anyone could see in a single visit. To help you prioritize your limited time and money, I've chosen—with much difficulty—what I think are the best of Paris' many sights. I've clustered them into walkable neighborhoods for more efficient sightseeing.

Definitely consider buying a Paris Museum Pass to save money and skip long ticket-buying lines, and review my other sightseeing tips (✪ see pages 207-208).

Note that some of Paris' biggest sights—the Louvre, the Eiffel Tower, and others—are described in much more detail in the individual self-guided tour chapters. There you'll also find crucial info on how to avoid lines, save money, and get a decent bite to eat nearby. If there's more information on a sight elsewhere, it's marked with a ✪.

HISTORIC CORE OF PARIS

The Historic Core consists of the island in the center of Paris named Ile de la Cité, and spills onto the neighboring river banks. Here you'll find sights from Paris' 2,000-year history, with an emphasis on its medieval glory days (Mo: Cité, Hôtel de Ville, or St. Michel).

▲▲▲Notre-Dame Cathedral (Cathédrale Notre-Dame de Paris)
The 850-year-old cathedral of "Our Lady" features winged gargoyles, flying buttresses, a climbable tower, and a solemn interior.
✪ See page 17 in the Historic Paris Walk chapter.

▲▲▲Sainte-Chapelle
Europe's best stained glass—and that's saying something!—makes this small Gothic church glow.
✪ See page 34 in the Historic Paris Walk chapter.

▲Conciergerie
Marie-Antoinette and thousands of others were imprisoned here on their way to the guillotine.
✪ See page 38 in the Historic Paris Walk chapter.

▲Deportation Memorial (Mémorial de la Déportation)
A sober remembrance of the 200,000 French victims of the Nazi concentration camps.
✪ See page 28 in the Historic Paris Walk chapter.

Paris Archaeological Crypt
Visit Roman ruins, trace the street plan of the medieval village, and see models of how early Paris grew. The ruins are a confusing mix of foundations from every time period, but interesting multimedia displays help sort them out: the city's oldest rampart, a medieval hospital, or a Roman building with a heated floor. Worthwhile if you have a Museum Pass.
▶ *€4, covered by Museum Pass, Tue-Sun 10:00-18:00, closed Mon, enter 100 yards in front of Notre-Dame, tel. 01 55 42 50 10.*

Sights

MAJOR MUSEUMS NEIGHBORHOOD

Paris' grandest park, the Tuileries Garden, links Paris' grandest museums. All these are less than a 20-minute walk apart. Key Métro stops are Palais Royal–Musée du Louvre, Concorde, and the RER-C stop called Musée d'Orsay.

▲▲▲Louvre (Musée du Louvre)
Europe's oldest, biggest, greatest, and most-crowded museum is home to *Mona Lisa, Venus de Milo,* and the rest of Western Civilization.
✪ See the Louvre Tour on page 43.

▲▲▲Orsay Museum (Musée d'Orsay)
Europe's greatest collection of Impressionism (Manet, Monet, Renoir), Post-Impressionism (Van Gogh, Cézanne, Gauguin), and more.
✪ See the Orsay Museum Tour on page 69.

▲▲Orangerie Museum (Musée de l'Orangerie)
Step out of the tree-lined, sun-dappled Impressionist painting that is the Tuileries Garden, and into the Orangerie (oh-rahn-zheh-ree), a little bijou of select works by Claude Monet and his contemporaries. Start with the

Orangerie—Monet's eight monumental canvases immerse you in his garden world of Giverny.

Sights

Major Museums Neighborhood

museum's claim to fame: Monet's water lilies. These eight mammoth-scale paintings are displayed exactly as Monet intended them—surrounding you in oval-shaped rooms—so you feel as though you're immersed in his garden at Giverny.

Working from his home there, Monet built a special studio with sky-lights and wheeled easels to accommodate the canvases—1,950 square feet in all. Each canvas features a different part of the pond, painted from varying angles at distinct times of day—but the true subject of these works is the play of reflected light off the surface of the pond. The Monet rooms are considered the first art installation, and the blurry canvases signaled the abstract art to come.

Downstairs you'll see artists that bridge the Impressionist and Modernist worlds—Renoir, Cézanne, Utrillo, Matisse, and Picasso. Together they provide a snapshot of what was hot in the world of art collecting, circa 1920.

▶ *€8, €5 after 17:00, covered by Museum Pass. Open Wed-Mon 9:00-18:00, closed Tue. English tours usually Mon and Thu at 14:30 and Sat at 11:00. It's located in the Tuileries Garden near Place de la Concorde, Mo: Concorde. Tel. 01 44 77 80 07, musee-orangerie.fr.*

Palais Royal Courtyards

Just steps from noisy Rue de Rivoli is this peaceful, perfectly Parisian scene—a courtyard of whimsical modern columns, flowers, outdoor cafés, and in-the-know Parisians walking their poodles, picnicking, and enjoying a rendezvous. At the far end, exit the courtyard to find traditional shopping arcades, which still bustle with shoppers.

▶ *Free and always open. It's directly north of the Louvre on Rue de Rivoli (Mo: Palais Royal–Musée du Louvre).*

EIFFEL TOWER AND NEARBY

From the Eiffel Tower to the golden dome of Invalides, this area has fine museums and the refined ambience of the Rue Cler. A number of Métro stops serve this neighborhood, but you may find the RER more useful.

▲▲▲Eiffel Tower (La Tour Eiffel)

The 1,000-foot tower was built as a tourist attraction, and it's still the must-see sight in Paris.

✪ See the Eiffel Tower Tour chapter on page 99.

▲▲Rodin Museum (Musée Rodin)

This user-friendly museum is filled with passionate works by the greatest sculptor since Michelangelo. You'll see *The Kiss, The Thinker,* the *Burghers of Calais, The Gates of Hell,* and many more. However, some rooms may be closed until the museum's renovation is complete in 2015.

Sights

Eiffel Tower & Nearby

Auguste Rodin (1840-1917) sculpted human figures on an epic scale, revealing through the body their deepest thoughts and feelings. Like many of Michelangelo's unfinished works, Rodin's statues rise from the raw stone around them, driven by the life force. With missing limbs and scarred skin, these are prefab classics, making ugliness noble. Rodin's people are always moving restlessly. Even the famous *Thinker* is moving. While he's plopped down solidly, his mind is a million miles away.

Rodin worked with many materials—he chiseled marble (though not often), modeled clay, cast bronze, worked plaster, painted, and sketched. He often created different versions of the same subject in different media.

Rodin lived and worked in this mansion, renting rooms alongside Henri Matisse, the poet Rainer Maria Rilke (Rodin's secretary), and the dancer Isadora Duncan. The well-displayed exhibits trace Rodin's artistic development and explain how his bronze statues were cast. Learn about Rodin's tumultuous relationship with his apprentice and lover, Camille Claudel, and see some of her passionate works done in a Rodin-esque style. And stroll the leafy gardens, dappled with many of his greatest works.

▶ €9, covered by Museum Pass, free on first Sun of the month. Open Tue-Sun 10:00-17:45, Wed until 20:45, closed Mon; gardens close at 18:00, Oct-March at 17:00; last entry 30 minutes before closing. It's near the golden dome of Invalides, 79 Rue de Varenne, Mo· Varenne. Tel. 01 44 18 61 10, musee-rodin.fr.

▲▲Army Museum and Napoleon's Tomb (Musée de l'Armée)

The Hôtel des Invalides—a former veterans' hospital topped by a golden dome—houses Napoleon's over-the-top-ornate tomb, as well as Europe's greatest military museum. Visiting the Army Museum's different sections, you can watch the art of war unfold from stone axes to Axis powers.

At the center of the complex, Napoleon Bonaparte lies majestically dead inside several coffins under a grand dome—a goose-bumping pilgrimage for historians. Your visit continues through an impressive range of museums filled with medieval armor, cannons and muskets, Louis XIV-era uniforms and weapons, and Napoleon's horse—stuffed and mounted.

The best section is dedicated to the two World Wars. Walk chronologically through displays on the trench warfare of WWI, France's horrendous losses, the victory parades, and the humiliating Treaty of Versailles that led to WWII. The WWII rooms use black-and-white photos, maps,

Rodin Museum—*The Kiss, The Thinker* and more   The Army Museum's WWII wing

videos, and a few artifacts to trace Hitler's rise, the Blitzkrieg that overran France, the concentration camps, America's entry into the war, D-Day, the atomic bomb, and the eventual Allied victory. There's special insight into France's role (the French Resistance), and how it was Charles de Gaulle who actually won the war.

▶ *€9.50 covers all museums and Napoleon's Tomb, €7.50 after 17:00, covered by Museum Pass.*

Museum open daily April-Sept 10:00-18:00, "Louis XIV to Napoleon I" wing open Tue until 21:00; Oct-March 10:00-17:00, closed first Mon of month Oct-June.

Tomb open daily April-June and Sept 10:00-18:00, open Tue until 21:00; July-Aug 10:00-19:00, may be open Tue until 21:00; Oct-March 10:00-17:00, closed first Mon of month Sept-May, last tickets sold 30 minutes before closing.

The Hôtel des Invalides is at 129 Rue de Grenelle; Mo: La Tour Maubourg, Varenne, or Invalides. Tel. 01 44 42 38 77 or toll 08 10 11 33 99, musee-armee.fr.

▲Paris Sewer Tour (Les Egouts de Paris)

Discover what happens after you flush. This quick, interesting, and slightly stinky visit takes you along a few hundred yards of water tunnels in the world's first and longest underground sewer system. With good English information, you'll trace the sewer's evolution: from Roman times to medieval (washed straight into the river), to Victor Hugo's fictional hero Jean Valjean (who hid here in *Les Misérables*), to today's 1,500 miles of tunnels carrying 317 million gallons of water a day. The sight has WCs.

▶ *€4.30, covered by Museum Pass. Open Sat-Wed May-Sept 11:00-17:00, Oct-April 11:00-16:00, closed Thu-Fri. Located at the south end of Pont de l'Alma, Mo: Alma-Marceau, RER: Pont de l'Alma. Tel. 01 53 68 27 81.*

▲▲Marmottan Museum (Musée Marmottan Monet)

This intimate, less-touristed mansion on the southwest fringe of urban Paris has the best collection of works by the father of Impressionism, Claude Monet (1840-1926). Fiercely independent and dedicated to his craft, Monet gave courage to the other Impressionists in the face of harsh criticism.

Though the museum is not arranged chronologically, you can trace his life. You'll see black-and-white sketches from his youth, his discovery

Best Views Over the City of Light

Eiffel Tower: The ultimate. Period.

Arc de Triomphe: Best at night when the Champs-Elysées positively glitters.

Notre-Dame's Tower: In the heart of Paris, among the gargoyles.

Steps of Sacré-Cœur: Join the guitar-strumming partiers on Paris' only hilltop (free).

Galeries Lafayette or Printemps: Both department stores have a stunning overlook of the old Opéra district (free).

Montparnasse Tower: This lone skyscraper's views are best by day.

Pompidou Center: Great views plus exciting modern art (free with Museum Pass).

Place du Trocadéro: It's at street level, but is the best place to see the Eiffel Tower (free). The Café Carlu is great for a drink.

Bar at Hôtel Concorde-Lafayette: This otherwise unappealing hotel has a 33rd-floor bar with a stunning night-time panorama (no cover charge, pricey drinks, 3 Place du Général Koenig, Mo: Porte Maillot, tel. 01 40 68 50 68, concorde-lafayette.com).

of open-air painting, and the canvas—*Impression: Sunrise*—that gave Impressionism its name. There are portraits of his wives and kids, and his well-known "series" paintings (done at different times of day) of London, Gare St. Lazare, and the Cathedral of Rouen. The museum's highlight is scenes from his garden at Giverny—the rose trellis, the Japanese bridge, and the larger-than-life water lilies.

In addition, the Marmottan features a world-class collection of works by Berthe Morisot and other Impressionists; an eclectic collection of non-Monet objects (furniture, illuminated manuscript drawings); and temporary exhibits.

▶ *€10, not covered by Museum Pass. Audioguide-€3. Open Tue-Sun 10:00-18:00, Thu until 20:00, closed Mon, last entry 30 minutes before closing. Located at 2 Rue Louis-Boilly, Mo: La Muette. Tel. 01 44 96 50 33, marmottan.fr.*

LEFT BANK

The Left Bank is as much an attitude as an actual neighborhood. There are fewer busy boulevards, businessmen in suits, and modern buildings, and more quiet lanes, students, and intimate cafés. The sightseeing core stretches roughly from the Panthéon to St. Germain-des-Prés, and from the river to Luxembourg Garden.

The part of the Left Bank called the **Latin Quarter** is just opposite Notre-Dame. This was medieval Paris' university district, where scholars spoke Latin. Historically, it has a reputation for artsy, bohemian character, though parts of it have become something of a tourist ghetto filled with cheap North African eateries. The neighborhood's main boulevards (St.

Michel and St. Germain) are lined with cafés—once the haunts of great poets and philosophers, and still popular today.

Lively nighttime hotspots on the Left Bank include areas around St Germain des-Prés Church, Rue de Buci, Rue des Canettes (near St. Sulpice), and the Latin Quarter. ✪ For boutique shopping, follow the route shown on the map on page 156.

▲▲Cluny Museum (Musée National du Moyen Age)

This treasure trove of art from the Middle Ages *(Moyen Age)* fills old Roman baths. You'll see the baths' cavernous cool-down room, plus displays of fine medieval objects: stained glass, swords, jewels, and the decapitated heads of Notre-Dame statues (✪ see page 22).

The star here is the exquisite *Lady and the Unicorn* series of six tapestries: A delicate, as-medieval-as-can be noble lady introduces a delighted unicorn to the senses of taste, hearing, sight, smell, and touch. The sixth is the most talked-about tapestry, called *A Mon Seul Désir* (To My Sole Desire). What *is* the lady's only desire? Is it that jewel box, or is it something—or someone—inside that tent? Middle Age Europe was awakening from a thousand-year slumber, Paris was emerging on the world stage, and the Renaissance was moving in like a warm front from Italy.

▶ *€8, free on first Sun of month, covered by Museum Pass, ticket includes audioguide (€1 for passholders). Open Wed-Mon 9:15-17:45, closed Tue, last entry at 17:15. Located at 6 Place Paul Painlevé, Mo: Cluny-La Sorbonne. Tel. 01 53 73 78 16, musee-moyenage.fr.*

▲St. Sulpice Church and Organ Concert

Sitting amid a colorful neighborhood of boutiques and cafés, this big but unremarkable church has several delights inside. Three murals of fighting angels by Delacroix (in the first chapel on the right) were completed during his final years, while fighting illness. They sum up his long career, from meticulously drawn Renaissance roots to furious Romanticism to messy-paint proto-Impressionism.

The Egyptian-style obelisk (on the wall of the north transept) is used as a sundial. The sun shines into the church through a tiny hole opposite the obelisk (high up on the south wall) and strikes a mark on the obelisk that indicates the date. (The sundial was featured in the novel *The Da Vinci Code*—a fanciful book that St. Sulpice's caretakers disdain.)

The church's organ is famous—7,000 pipes, five keyboards, and

Head to the Cluny Museum for medieval art.

Luxembourg Garden—an urban oasis

powered by a clutch of bellows-pumpers. The 300-year tradition of great organists continues today. Every Sunday, the 10:30-11:30 Mass (come appropriately dressed) is followed by a high-powered 25-minute recital by current organist Daniel Roth.

▶ *Free, open daily 7:30-19:30, Mo: St. Sulpice or Mabillon. For organ concerts, see stsulpice.com.*

▲Luxembourg Garden (Jardin du Luxembourg)

Slip into a green chair by the pond and take in the Impressionist scene around you—the radiant flower beds, the old men playing chess, kids sailing toy boats...the joggers on cell phones. The 60-acre gardens are dotted with fountains and statues and anchored by the Renaissance-style Luxembourg Palace, where the French Senate meets. The brilliant flower beds are completely changed three times a year, and the boxed trees are brought out of the *orangerie* in May. Children enjoy pony rides and marionette shows (Les Guignols, or Punch and Judy). There's no better place to watch Parisians at play.

▶ *Open daily dawn until dusk, Mo: Odéon, RER: Luxembourg.*

▲Panthéon

This state-capitol-style Neoclassical monument celebrates France's illustrious history. Built to be a church, it was converted during the Revolution (1791) into a secular mausoleum honoring "the great men of the Fatherland."

Inside the vast building (360' by 280' by 270'), monuments trace the triumphs of the French people. Foucault's pendulum (first placed here in 1851) still swings gracefully at the end of a 220-foot cable, demonstrating how the earth rotates beneath it. Downstairs in the crypt lies a pantheon of greats—the tombs of philosophers Rousseau and Voltaire, scientist Marie Curie, and writers Victor Hugo and Alexandre Dumas. You can climb up the dome for fine views (dome access may be closed for renovation).

▶ *€8, covered by Museum Pass. Open daily 10:00-18:30 in summer, until 18:00 in winter, last entry 45 minutes before closing. Escorted dome visits leave hourly. Mo: Cardinal Lemoine. Tel. 01 44 32 18 00, pantheon .monuments-nationaux.fr.*

Montparnasse Tower (La Tour Montparnasse)

This ugly, out-of-place, 59-story superscraper has one virtue—its view. It's cheaper and easier to visit than the Eiffel Tower, the view includes the Eiffel Tower...and you can't see the Montparnasse Tower at all. Sunset is great, but views are disappointing after dark. The 56th floor has a restaurant (reasonable for drinks or light lunch), exhibits identifying the monuments below, and a worthwhile 12-minute video. Then climb to the 59th-floor helipad—690 feet above Paris—and scan the city with the wind in your hair.

▶ *€13, possible discount with this book, not covered by Museum Pass. April-Sept daily 9:30-23:30; Oct-March daily 9:30-22:30, Fri-Sat until 23:00; last entry 30 minutes before closing. Enter on Rue de l'Arrivée, Mo: Montparnasse-Bienvenüe (follow signs for* La Tour). *Tel. 01 45 38 52 56, tourmontparnasse56.com.*

▲Catacombs

Descend 60 feet below the street and walk a one-mile, one-hour route through tunnels containing the anonymous bones of six million permanent Parisians.

In 1786, a health-conscious city emptied the church cemeteries and moved the bones here, to former limestone quarries. The bones are stacked in piles 5 feet high and as much as 80 feet deep. Ignore the sign announcing, "Halt, this is the empire of the dead," and walk through passageways of skull-studded tibiae, past more cheery signs: "Happy is he who is forever faced with the hour of his death and prepares himself for the end every day." You emerge far from where you entered, with white-limestone-covered toes, telling everyone you've been underground gawking at bones. Note to wannabe Hamlets: An attendant checks your bag at the exit for stolen souvenirs.

▶ *€8, not covered by Museum Pass. Open Tue-Sun 10:00-17:00, closed Mon, last entry at 16:00. Located at 1 Place Denfert-Rochereau, Mo:*

Denfert-Rochereau. You'll exit at 36 Rue Remy Dumoncel; turn right and walk several blocks to either Mo: Alésia or Mouton Duvernet. Tel. 01 43 22 47 63. Expect a one-hour wait in line—arrive by 14:30 or risk not getting in. A flashlight is handy. Being under 6'2" is helpful.

CHAMPS-ELYSÉES AND NEARBY

This famous boulevard is Paris' backbone, stretching from the Arc de Triomphe downhill to Place de la Concorde. The surrounding area features more broad boulevards lined with big, classy 19th-century buildings. These days, the boulevards are choked with cars, and the buildings house the glitzy businesses of globalized Paris.

▲▲Champs-Elysées

The Champs-Elysées is as international as it is Parisian, and a walk down the two-mile boulevard is a must.

In 1667, Louis XIV opened the first section of the street, and it soon became *the* place to cruise in your carriage. (It still is today.) By the 1920s, this boulevard was pure elegance—fancy residences, rich hotels, and cafés. Today it's home to big business, celebrity cafés, glitzy nightclubs, high-fashion shopping, and international people-watching. People gather here to celebrate Bastille Day (July 14), World Cup triumphs, and the finale of the Tour de France.

Start at the Arc de Triomphe (Mo: Charles de Gaulle-Etoile) and head downhill on the left-hand side. The arrival of McDonald's (at #140) was an unthinkable horror, but these days dining *chez MacDo* has become typically Parisian, and this branch is the most profitable McDonald's in the world.

Fancy car showrooms abound, including Peugeot (#136) and Mercedes-Benz (#118). The Lido (#116) is Paris' largest burlesque-type cabaret (and a multiplex cinema). Across the boulevard is the flagship store of leather-bag makers Louis Vuitton (#101). Fouquet's café (#99), is a popular spot for French celebrities, especially movie stars—note the names in the sidewalk in front. Enter if you dare for an €8 espresso. Ladurée café (#75) is also classy but has a welcoming and affordable take-out bakery.

Continuing on, you pass international-brand stores, such as Sephora perfume, Virgin, Disney, the Gap, etc. You can end your walk at the round

---

Champs-Elysées & Nearby

Rond Point intersection (Mo: Franklin D. Roosevelt) or continue to obelisk-studded Place de la Concorde, Paris' largest square.

▲▲▲Arc de Triomphe

Napoleon built the magnificent Arc de Triomphe to commemorate his victory at the battle of Austerlitz. There's no triumphal arch bigger—165 feet high, 130 feet wide. The carvings show a toga-clad Napoleon (left pillar) and an excitable Lady Liberty leading the people (right).

Beneath the Arch is the Tomb of the Unknown Soldier where, every day at 18:30, the flame is rekindled and new flowers set in place. The foot of the arch is a stage on which the last two centuries of Parisian history have played out—from the funeral of Napoleon to the goose-stepping arrival of the Nazis to the triumphant return of Charles de Gaulle after the Allied liberation. Today, national parades start and end here with one minute of silence.

Enter and climb the 284 steps to the observation deck up top, with sweeping skyline panoramas. You're at the center of a grand axis of city planning, stretching from the Louvre, up the Champs-Elysées to the Arc de

Champs-Elysees with Arc de Triomphe   Opera Garnier's grand staircase

Triomphe, then continuing west to the huge rectangular, modern Grande Arche de la Défense.

Looking down you see 12 converging boulevards forming a star *(etoile)*. What a traffic mess! Or is it? Cars entering the circle have the right of way, blending in smoothly while others jockey to the perimeter to exit. Still, there are plenty of accidents, and insurance companies—tired of the disputes—routinely split the damages 50/50.

▶ *€9.50 to climb, free on first Sun of month Oct-March, covered by Museum Pass. Open daily April-Sept 10:00-23:00, Oct-March 10:00-22:30, last entry 45 minutes before closing. Use the underpass to reach the arch. Mo: Charles de Gaulle-Etoile. Tel. 01 55 37 73 77, arc-de-triomphe .monuments-nationaux.fr.*

▲Opéra Garnier

This grand theater (1875) of France's beautiful age—the belle époque—still anchors a neighborhood filled with Paris' most fashionable haunts.

The building is huge, though the auditorium itself seats only 2,000. There's a cavernous backstage to accommodate elaborate sets, as well as the extravagant lobbies out front. That's where the real show took place, between acts, when the elite of Paris—out to see and be seen—strutted their elegant stuff. The massive foundations straddle an underground lake, inspiring the mysterious world of the *Phantom of the Opera.*

Visitors can explore the lobbies, the grand marble staircase, and the Salon du Glacier, iced with decor typical of 1900. The small museum will interest opera buffs. The highlight of the visit is a view from the upper seats into the actual red-velvet performance hall. There you can see Marc Chagall's colorful ceiling (1964) and an eight-ton chandelier.

These days, most opera is performed across town at the modern and functional Bastille Opera House. But the Garnier still hosts ballets and concerts, and attending a performance—dressed in the cleanest clothes you can find in your rucksack—can transport you back to the belle époque.

▶ *€9, not covered by Museum Pass. Erratic opening hours due to performances and rehearsals, but generally daily 10:00-16:30, mid-July-Aug until 18:00. Located at 8 Rue Scribe, Mo. Opéra. €13.50 English tours run daily during summer (off-season on weekends and Wed) usually at 11:30 and 14:30—call to confirm. Tel. 01 40 01 17 89 or 08 25 05 44 05.*

For performances (generally Oct-June), check the schedule and buy tickets at the box office; by phone at tel. 08 92 89 90 90 or (from the US) tel. 011 33 1 71 25 24 23; or online at operadeparis.fr.

Near the Opéra are the Fragonard Perfume Museum (free, 9 Rue Scribe), the venerable Galeries Lafayette department store (40 Boulevard Haussmann), and the glitterati-flecked Café de la Paix (Place de l'Opéra).

▲Petit Palais (and its Musée des Beaux-Arts)

Besides its always-interesting temporary exhibits (which charge for admission), this museum has a free permanent collection of pretty-good 19th-century paintings and much more.

Enter the museum, ask for a ticket to the permanent collection (free but required), and head toward the left wing, filled with turn-of-the-century vases and portraits. The main hall has Courbet's soft-porn *The Sleepers* (*Le Sommeil*, 1866), capturing two women nestled in post-climactic bliss. At the end of the main hall, enter the smaller room to find Claude Monet's hazy, moody *Sunset on the Seine at Lavacourt* (1880), painted the winter after his wife died. Nearby are works by the American painter Mary Cassatt and other Impressionists. Downstairs, there's an eclectic mix of Greek antiquities and Art Nouveau. The Palais also has a pleasant garden courtyard and café.

Across the street from the Petit Palais is the **Grand Palais**—an exhibition hall built for the 1900 World's Fair that's now used for temporary exhibits (see grandpalais.fr).

▶ *The Petit Palais is free. Open Tue-Sun 10:00-18:00, Thu until 20:00 for temporary exhibits, closed Mon. Located on Avenue Winston Churchill, Mo: Champs-Elysées-Clemenceau. Tel. 01 53 43 40 00, petitpalais .paris.fr.*

▲▲Jacquemart-André Museum (Musée Jacquemart-André)

This thoroughly enjoyable museum certainly has some nice art, but its star is the lavish mansion itself—an intimate look at the lifestyle of a wealthy, art-loving 19th-century couple. Edouard André and his wife Nélie Jacquemart had no children. They spent their lives and fortunes designing, building, and then decorating this sumptuous mansion—strewn with enough paintings by Rembrandt, Botticelli, Uccello, Mantegna, Bellini, Boucher, and Fragonard to make a painting gallery famous. The included audioguide is excellent, and the museum's sumptuous tearoom serves delicious cakes and tea. A few blocks north is Paris' most beautiful park, Parc Monceau.

▸ *€11, not covered by Museum Pass, daily 10:00-18:00. Located at 158 Boulevard Haussmann, Mo: Miromesnil or Saint-Philippe de Roule. Tel. 01 45 62 11 59, musee-jacquemart-andre.com.*

MARAIS NEIGHBORHOOD AND MORE

The Marais neighborhood extends along the Right Bank of the Seine, from the Pompidou Center to the Bastille. There's a main west–east axis formed by Rue Ste. Croix de la Bretonnerie, Rue des Rosiers (heart of Paris' Jewish community), and Rue St. Antoine. The centerpiece of the neighborhood is the elegant Place des Vosges. Helpful Métro stops are Bastille, Saint-Paul, and Hôtel de Ville.

▲Strolling the Marais

With more pre-Revolutionary lanes and mansions than anywhere else in town, the Marais is more atmospheric than touristy. In the 1600s, this former swamp *(marais)* became home to aristocrats' private mansions *(hôtels),* located close to the king's townhouse on stylish Place des Vosges. With the Revolution, the Marais turned working-class, filled with artisans and immigrants, and became home to Paris' Jewish community. Today the area is trending upward and becoming home to young professionals.

For a good east-to-west introductory walk, start at Place de la Bastille (nightlife) and head west on busy Rue Saint-Antoine to Place des Vosges (art galleries, restaurants). Continue west on Rue des Francs Bourgeois (fashion boutiques), turning onto Rue des Rosiers (Jewish neighborhood) and Rue Ste. Croix de la Bretonnerie (gay Paree's LGBT community). On Sunday afternoons, the area pulses with shoppers and café crowds.

Marais Neighborhood & Nearby

▲Place des Vosges

Henry IV (r. 1589-1610) built this centerpiece of the Marais in 1605, instantly turning the Marais into Paris' most exclusive neighborhood. In the center, a statue of Louis XIII on horseback gestures, "Look at this wonderful square my dad built." He's surrounded by locals in the shade of trees, children frolicking in the sandbox, lovers warming benches, and pigeons guarding their fountains. Around the square, arcades shade cafés and art galleries.

Study the architecture: nine pavilions (houses) per side. The two highest—at the front and back—were intended for the king and queen, but were never used. Warm red brickwork—some real, some fake—is topped with sloped slate roofs, chimneys, and another quaint relic of a bygone era: TV antennas.

At 6 Place des Vosges is **Victor Hugo's House,** a free museum dedicated to France's literary giant (1802-1885). Hugo lived here after the phenomenal success of *The Hunchback of Notre-Dame* and while he was writing *Les Misérables* (open Tue-Sun 10:00-18:00, musee-hugo.paris.fr).

Place de la Bastille

Although this vast square is the former site of the infamous prison that was stormed on July 14, 1789, sparking the French Revolution, the building is long gone, and only a tall memorial column marks the spot.

▲Rue des Rosiers—Jewish Quarter

Once the largest in Western Europe, Paris' Jewish Quarter is still colorful. The intersection of Rue des Rosiers and Rue des Ecouffes marks the heart of the small neighborhood that Jews call the Pletzl ("little place").

Rue des Rosiers features kosher *(cascher)* restaurants and fast-food places selling falafel, *shawarma, kefta,* and other Mediterranean dishes. Bakeries specialize in braided challah, bagels, and strudels. Delis offer gefilte fish, piroshkis, and blintzes. Art galleries exhibit Jewish-themed works, and store windows post flyers for community events. Need a menorah? This is a great place to buy one. You may see Jewish men in yarmulkes, a few bearded Orthodox Jews, and Hasidic Jews with black coat and hat, beard, and earlocks.

▶ *Though some Jewish shops close on Saturday (the Jewish Sabbath), the Marais is liveliest on weekends.*

▲▲Pompidou Center (Centre Pompidou)

Some people hate Modern art. But Paris was the cradle of Modernism, and the Pompidou houses one of Europe's greatest collections. In addition, the Pompidou Center always has lively temporary exhibitions, the rooftop has a great view, and outside there's a perpetual street fair of performers and crepe stands.

The colorful building is exoskeletal (like a crab or Notre-Dame), with its functional parts—the pipes, heating ducts, and escalator—on the outside, and the meaty art inside. It's the epitome of Modern architecture, where "form follows function."

Rue des Rosiers draws Jewish shoppers.

Pompidou—wild and crazy modern art

The permanent collection (on the fourth and fifth floors) features all the big names of the early 20th century—Matisse, Picasso, Chagall, Kandinsky, Dalí—and continues with post 1960 art. This art was ahead of its time and is still waiting for the world to catch up. After so many Madonnas-and-children in Paris' older museums, a piano smashed to bits and glued to the wall is refreshing. Once you've seen the permanent collection, explore the temporary exhibits to connect with what is "now" from around the globe.

▶ *€11-13 depending on current exhibits, free on first Sun of month. The Museum Pass covers the permanent collection and view escalators but not special exhibitions. €3 for view only.*

Open Wed-Mon 11:00-21:00, closed Tue, ticket counters close at 20:00. Located at Mo: Rambuteau or Hôtel de Ville. Tel. 01 44 78 12 33, centrepompidou.fr.

▲Jewish Art and History Museum (Musée d'Art et Histoire du Judaïsme)

This fine museum in a Marais mansion tells the story of Judaism in Europe and the traditions that helped the dispersed population maintain cultural unity. Besides learning about bar mitzvahs and menorahs, you'll see exquisite traditional costumes and objects, and paintings by Jewish artists such as Chagall, Modigliani, and Soutine.

▶ *€7, includes audioguide, covered by Museum Pass. Open Sun-Fri 11:00-18:00, closed Sat, last entry 45 minutes before closing. 71 Rue du Temple, Mo: Rambuteau. Tel. 01 53 01 86 60, mahj.org.*

▲▲Picasso Museum (Musée Picasso)

The 20th century's most famous and—OK, I'll say it—greatest artist was the master of many styles (Cubism, Surrealism, Expressionism, etc.) and of many media (painting, sculpture, prints, ceramics, and assemblages). Still, he could make anything he touched look unmistakably like "a Picasso."

The recently renovated Picasso Museum (reopening by summer 2014) has the world's largest collection of Picasso's work—some 400 works, spread across four levels of this mansion in the Marais. A visit here walks you through the full range of this complex man's life and art.

Born in Spain, Picasso (1881-1973) was the prodigious son of an art teacher. In 1900, the brash Spaniard moved to Paris, the undisputed world capital of culture. Poor and homesick, he entered his "Blue Period," painting emaciated beggars, hard-eyed pimps, and himself, bundled up against the cold.

In 1904, Picasso moved into his Bateau-Lavoir studio on Montmartre, got a steady girlfriend, and suddenly saw the world through rose-colored glasses—the Rose Period. With his neighbor, Georges Braque, Picasso invented Cubism, fracturing a figure into a barely recognizable jumble of "cube"-like facets. In a few short years, Picasso had turned painting in the direction it would go for the next five decades.

After World War I, Picasso moved to the Montparnasse neighborhood, immersing himself in Paris' rich cultural life. In 1940, Nazi tanks rolled into Paris. Picasso's war-era paintings are gray and bleak.

At war's end, Picasso left Paris for the sunny skies of the French Riviera. He was reborn, enjoying worldwide fame and the love of a woman a third his age (Picasso had a number of wives/girlfriends/Muses over the years—the museum has several of their portraits). Picasso's Riviera works are bright, lighthearted, and childlike, featuring new media (especially pottery) and motifs of the sea. He was fertile to the end, still painting with bright thick colors at age 91.

▶ *€10, covered by Museum Pass, additional fee for temporary exhibits. Reopening by summer 2014. Likely open daily 9:00-19:30, some Sat until 22:00, last entry 45 minutes before closing; 5 Rue de Thorigny, Mo: St. Paul or Chemin Vert, tel. 01 42 71 25 21, musee-picasso.fr.*

▲Carnavalet Museum (Musée Carnavalet)

At the Carnavalet Museum, French history unfolds in a series of stills—like a Ken Burns documentary, except you have to walk. The Revolution is the highlight, but you get a good overview of everything—from Louis XIV period rooms to Napoleon to the belle époque.

The Revolution section is the best. No period of history is as charged with the full range of human drama: bloodshed, martyrdom, daring speeches, murdered priests, emancipated women, backstabbing former friends—all in the name of government "by, for, and of the people."

You'll see paintings of the Estates General assembly that planted the seeds of democracy. Then comes a model of the Bastille, the hated prison that was the symbol of oppression. Read the "Declaration of the Rights of Man." Find pictures of ill-fated King Louis XVI and Queen Marie-Antoinette, and the fate that awaited them—the guillotine. You'll see portraits of all the major players—Robespierre, Danton, Charlotte Corday—as well as the dashing general who would inherit democracy and turn it into dictatorship... Napoleon Bonaparte.

▸ *Free, audioguide-€5. Open Tue-Sun 10:00-18:00, closed Mon. Located at 23 Rue de Sévigné, Mo: St. Paul. Tel. 01 44 59 58 58, carnavalet .paris.fr.*

▲Père Lachaise Cemetery (Cimetière du Père Lachaise)

This 100-acre cemetery is big and confusing, but it's a pleasant park-like setting for a stroll. Find the graves of illustrious people who have called Paris home: Frédéric Chopin (the Polish pianist whose tomb always sports fresh flowers), Molière (playwright to Louis XIV), Edith Piaf (warbling singer who regretted nothing), Oscar Wilde (controversial figure who died in Paris), Jim Morrison (ditto), Gertrude Stein (American writer), Héloïse and Abélard (illicit medieval lovers), and many more.

▸ *Free, open Mon-Fri 8:00-18:00, Sat 8:30-18:00, Sun 9:00-18:00, closes at 17:30 in winter, last entry 15 minutes before closing. Buy grave-locator maps from shops near the entrance. The best entrance is Porte Gambetta near Mo: Gambetta (not Mo: Père Lachaise) and bus #69's last stop. Tel. 01 55 25 82 10, map available at unofficial website: pere -lachaise.com.*

▲Montmartre

Paris' highest hill, topped by Sacré-Cœur Basilica, is best known as the home of cabaret nightlife and bohemian artists. Struggling painters, poets, dreamers, and drunkards came here for cheap rent, untaxed booze, rustic landscapes, and views of the underwear of high-kicking cancan girls at the Moulin Rouge. These days, the hill is equal parts charm and kitsch—still

Chopin's grave at Pere Lachaise Cemetery

Montmartre, capped with Sacré-Cœur

vaguely village-like but mobbed with tourists and pickpockets on sunny weekends. Come for a bit of history, a get-away from Paris' noisy boulevards, and the view.

Start your visit at the Sacré-Cœur (Sacred Heart) Basilica. The striking exterior, with its onion domes and bleached-bone pallor, looks ancient, but was finished only a century ago. Inside, a mosaic shows Jesus with his sacred heart burning with love for mankind. For an unobstructed panoramic view of Paris, climb 260 feet (300 steps) up the tight and claustrophobic spiral stairs to the top of the dome (church is free, open daily 6:00-22:30; dome costs €6, not covered by Museum Pass, open daily May-Sept 9:00-19:00, Oct-April 9:00-17:00; tel 01 53 41 89 00, sacre-coeur-montmartre.com).

Nearby is the leafy Place du Tertre, the heart of the hilltop neighborhood. Lined with restaurants and filled with draw-your-portrait artists, this was once the haunt of Toulouse-Lautrec and the original bohemians. Today, it's mobbed with tourists and unoriginal bohemians, but it's still fun. A block west is a *boulangerie* made famous in a painting by Utrillo. Head downhill past a vineyard to the Montmartre Museum, housed in a mansion that both Renoir and Utrillo once called home. The museum re-creates the cabaret scene, with paintings, original posters, and memorabilia (€8, not covered by Museum Pass, open daily 10:00-18:00, 12 Rue Cortot, tel. 01 49 25 89 39, museedemontmartre.fr).

A few blocks away are the historic Au Lapin Agile cabaret (still in business) and the Moulin de la Galette, a dance hall featured in a famous Renoir painting (✪ see page 86). Wandering the neighborhood, you can see the (boring) exteriors of former homes of Picasso, Toulouse-Lautrec, Van Gogh, and Erik Satie.

At the base of the hill (near Mo: Blanche), the Moulin Rouge ("Red

A Page of History

The Beginnings (A.D.1-1500): Julius Caesar conquered the Parisii, turning Paris from a tribal fishing village into a European city. The mix of Latin (southern) and Celtic (northern) cultures, with Paris right in the middle, defined the French character. Roman Paris fell to the Franks (hence "France") and Norsemen ("Normans"). Charlemagne (768-814) briefly united the Franks, giving a glimpse of modern France.

In 1066, William the Conqueror awkwardly united England and France, bringing centuries of border wars. Eventually, the teenage visionary Joan of Arc (1412 1431) rallied the French to drive the English out. Modern France was born.

France Dominates (1500-1789): Renaissance kings François I and Henry IV established France as a European power, and Louis XIV made it a superpower. Under Louis XV and XVI, every educated European spoke French and followed French aristocratic customs. Meanwhile, enlightened French philosophers sowed the seeds of democracy.

Revolution: (1789-1800): On July 14, 1789, Parisian revolutionaries stormed the Bastille, and eventually beheaded the king and queen. Thousands were guillotined if suspected of hindering democracy's march. From the chaos rose a charismatic commoner: Napoleon Bonaparte.

Elected Emperors and Constitutional Kings (1800s): Napoleon conquered Europe, crowned himself emperor, and invaded Russia, before being defeated at Waterloo. The monarchy was restored, but rulers had to toe the democratic line. Eventually, Napoleon's nephew (Napoleon III) presided over a wealthy-but-declining era of big monuments and Impressionist art, known as the belle époque—the "beautiful age."

War and Depression (1900-1950): Two world wars with Germany wasted the country. France lost millions of men in World War I and was easily overrun by Hitler in World War II. Paris, now dirt cheap, attracted foreign writers (Hemingway) and artists (Picasso).

Postwar France (1950-Present): France recovered slowly under wartime hero Charles de Gaulle. As its colonial empire dissolved after bitter wars in Algeria and Vietnam, immigrants flooded Paris. The turbulent '60s, progressive '70s, socialist-turned-conservative '80s, and the middle-of-the-road '90s brought us to the 21st century. Paris has regained its place as one of the world's great cities.

Sights

Windmill") nightclub still offers glitzy, pricey shows to busloads of tourists. The neighborhood around it, called Pigalle, is pretty rough and raunchy, with sex shops and bars where a €150 bottle of cheap champagne comes with a friend.

▶ *The Anvers Métro stop takes you to the base of the hill, where you can climb stairs up or ride a funicular. The Abbesses stop is closer but less scenic. From Place Pigalle, the "Montmartobus" (a public city bus) travels to many popular stops atop the hill. A taxi to the top costs about €15 from Notre-Dame.*

DAY TRIPS FROM PARIS

Though there's plenty to see within Paris' ring-road, efficient public transportation expands your sightseeing horizons.

▲▲▲Versailles
Twelve miles southwest of Paris, the jaw-dropping residence of French kings features a lavish palace and expansive, fountain-dotted gardens.

▶ ✪ *See the Versailles chapter on page 121.*

▲▲Chartres: The Town and the Cathedral
One of Europe's greatest Gothic cathedrals soars above the pleasant town of Chartres, an hour southwest of Paris.

▶ *Catch the train from Paris' Gare Montparnasse (10/day, about €13 one-way). The church is free and open daily 8:30-19:30.*

▲Giverny
Claude Monet's garden still looks like it did when he painted it. Wander among the flowers, the rose trellis, the Japanese Bridge, and the pond filled with lily pads.

▶ *Big bus tours are the easiest way to get there (about €70, ask your hotelier). On your own, take the Rouen-bound train from Gare St. Lazare to Vernon (about €25 round-trip, 45 minutes). From there, take a taxi (€12), the public bus, or rent a bike at the café opposite the train station (€14). Monet's Garden and House are open daily April-Oct 9:30-18:00, last entry 17:30, closed Nov-March (€9, not covered by Museum Pass, tel. 02 32 51 90 31, fondation-monet.com).*

Sleeping

In Paris, choosing the right neighborhood is as important as choosing the right hotel. I've focused most of my recommendations in three safe, handy, and colorful neighborhoods: the village-like Rue Cler (near the Eiffel Tower), the artsy and trendy Marais (near Place de la Bastille), and the lively yet classy Luxembourg (on the Left Bank). I like hotels that are clean, central, good-value, friendly, run with a respect for French traditions, and small enough to have a hands-on owner and stable staff. Four of these six virtues means it's a keeper.

Double rooms listed in this book average around €150 (including a private bathroom). They range from a low of roughly €70 (very simple, with toilet and shower down the hall) to €500 (maximum plumbing and more).

A Typical Parisian Hotel Room

A typical €150 double room in Paris will be small by American standards. It will have one double bed (either queen-sized or slightly narrower) or two twins. There's probably a bathroom in the room with a toilet, sink, and bathtub or shower. The room has a telephone and TV, and may have a safe. Most hotels at this price will have air-conditioning—cheaper places may not. Single rooms, triples, and quads will have similar features.

Breakfast is rarely included in the room price, but is usually offered for an additional €8-15. It's normally a self-service buffet of cereal, cheese, yogurt, fruit, and juice, while a waitress takes your coffee order.

The hotel will have Internet access, either Wi-Fi or a public terminal in the lobby. Though there may be a charge, at many of my listings, at least one of these options is free. The staff speaks at least enough English to get by. Night clerks aren't paid enough to care deeply about problems that arise.

Note that the French hotel rating system (zero to five stars) only reflects the number of amenities (e.g., fancier lobbies, more elaborately designed rooms), and does not necessarily rate quality. I rarely pay attention to it when choosing a hotel.

Making Reservations

Reserve months in advance, or as soon as you've pinned down your travel dates, particularly if you'll be traveling during peak season (April-Oct, especially May, June, Sept, and Oct) or for a major holiday. Do it by phone, through the hotel's website, or with an email that reads something like this:

Dear Hotel Magnifique,

I would like to reserve a double room for 2 people for 3 nights, arriving 19 July and departing 22 July. If possible, I would like a quiet room with a double bed (not twin beds), air-conditioning, and a shower (not a tub). Please let me know if you have a room available and the price. Thank you.

If they require your credit-card number for a deposit, you can send it by email (I do), but it's safer via phone, the hotel's secure website, or split between two emails. Once your room is booked, print out the confirmation, and reconfirm your reservation with a phone call or email a day or two in advance (alert them if you'll be arriving after 17:00). If canceling a reservation, some hotels require advance notice—otherwise they may bill you. Even if there's no penalty, it's polite to give at least three days' notice.

Hotel Price Code

$$$	Most rooms are €200 or more.
$$	Most rooms between €150-200.
$	Most rooms €150 or less.

These ranges cover rates for a standard double room with bath during high season. Asterisks (*) are for the French hotel rating system, ranging from zero to five stars. All hotels listed have an elevator, air conditioning (A/C), and Wi-Fi unless otherwise noted. For the best prices, book direct.

Budget Tips

To get the best rates, book directly with the hotel, not through a hotel-booking engine. Start with the hotel's website, looking for promo deals. Check rates every few days, as prices can vary greatly based on demand. Email several hotels to ask for their best price and compare offers—you may be astonished at the range. Some of my listed hotels offer a "Rick Steves discount" for readers of this book—it's worth asking when you reserve. Hotels farther from the Seine are cheaper (but less atmospheric or convenient).

Besides hotels, there are cheaper alternatives. I list a few all-ages hostels, which offer €25-35 dorm beds (and a few inexpensive doubles) and come with curfews and other rules. Bed-and-breakfasts (B&Bs) offer a personal touch at a fair price—try bed-and-breakfast-in-paris.com. Airbnb.com makes it reasonably easy to find a place to sleep in someone's home.

Renting an apartment can save money if you're traveling as a family, staying more than a week, and planning to cook your own meals. Try homeaway.com (offering a wide range of listings), parisperfect.com or parisforrent.com (specializing in top-end apartments), localflat.com (from tiny studios to multi-bedroom flats), francehomestyle.com (personalized service), homerental.fr (no agency fees), or vrbo.com (putting you directly in touch with owners).

Don't be too cheap when picking a place to stay. Choose a nice, central neighborhood. In summer, pay a little more for air-conditioning. Your Paris experience will be more memorable with a welcoming oasis to call home.

RUE CLER AREA—A safe, tidy, upscale area near the Eiffel Tower; Metro stops Ecole Militaire, La Tour Maubourg, and Invalides

$$$ Hôtel Relais Bosquet*** 19 Rue du Champ de Mars tel. 01 47 05 25 45 hotel-paris-bosquet.com	Fine hotel with generous public spaces and large, comfortable rooms, RS discount
$$$ Hôtel du Cadran*** 10 Rue du Champ de Mars tel. 01 40 62 67 00 cadranhotel.com	Perfectly located, daringly modern with stylish rooms, RS discount
$$$ Hôtel Valadon** 16 Rue Valadon tel. 01 47 53 89 85 hotelvaladon.com	Cute and quiet with 12 pleasing rooms, near Rue Cler, RS discount
$$ Hôtel Beaugency*** 21 Rue Duvivier tel. 01 47 05 01 63 hotel-beaugency.com	Good value on quiet street near Rue Cler, small rooms, RS discount
$$ Grand Hôtel Lévêque** 29 Rue Cler tel. 01 47 05 49 15 hotel-leveque.com	Busy hotel with average rooms right on Rue Cler
$ Hôtel du Champ de Mars** 7 Rue du Champ de Mars tel. 01 45 51 52 30 hotelduchampdemars.com	Plush little hotel with serious owners, snug but lovingly kept rooms, no A/C
$$$ Hôtel Duquesne Eiffel*** 23 Avenue Duquesne tel. 01 44 42 09 09 hde.fr	Hospitable and expertly run with handsome rooms and welcoming lobby, RS discount
$ Hôtel Eiffel Turenne** 20 Avenue de Tourville tel. 01 47 05 99 92 hotel-turenne-paris.com	Humble but well-situated with adequate rooms and several true single rooms

$$$ Hôtel de Londres Eiffel*** 1 Rue Augereau tel. 01 45 51 63 02 londres-eiffel.com	Close to Eiffel Tower with immaculate, warmly decorated rooms and helpful staff
$ Hôtel de la Tour Eiffel** 17 Rue de l'Exposition tel. 01 47 05 14 75 hotel-toureiffel.com	Fair value, quiet street, modest rooms, thin walls, no A/C, no breakfast
$ Hôtel Kensington** 79 Avenue de la Bourdonnais tel. 01 47 05 74 00 hotel-kensington.com	Good budget hotel near Eiffel Tower, small rooms, no A/C, no Wi-Fi
$$$ Hôtel Les Jardins d'Eiffel*** 8 Rue Amélie tel. 01 47 05 46 21 hoteljardinseiffel.com	Modern hotel with spacious and peaceful rooms and comfortable lobby, RS discount
$$$ Hôtel Muguet*** 11 Rue Chevert tel. 01 47 05 05 93 hotelmuguet.com	Peaceful refuge with tasteful rooms and garden courtyard; strict cancellation policy
$$$ Hôtel de l'Empereur** 2 Rue Chevert tel. 01 45 55 88 02 hotelempereurparis.com	Smashing views of Invalides from plush rooms; strict cancellation policy

MARAIS AREA—Classy mansions alongside trendy boutiques create a Greenwich Village vibe; Metro stops Bastille, Saint-Paul, and Hôtel de Ville

$$ Hôtel Castex*** 5 Rue Castex tel. 01 42 72 31 52 castexhotel.com	Quiet street, comfortable but narrow, tile-floored rooms, family suites
$$ Hôtel Bastille Spéria*** 1 Rue de la Bastille tel. 01 42 72 04 01 hotelsperia.com	Ideally located business-class hotel with modern, well-configured rooms

$$ Hôtel du 7ème Art** 20 Rue St. Paul tel. 01 44 54 85 00 paris-hotel-7art.com	Carefree with spacious rooms and 1970s decor, no elevator, smoking OK in all rooms
$ Hôtel Jeanne d'Arc** 3 Rue de Jarente tel. 01 48 87 62 11 hoteljeannedarc.com	Lovely little hotel with thoughtfully appointed rooms, great location, no A/C
$ Hôtel Daval** 21 Rue Daval tel. 01 47 00 51 23 hoteldaval.com	Small rooms, narrow halls, and good rates; streetside rooms can be loud
$ MIJE Fourcy 6 Rue de Fourcy tel. 01 42 74 23 45 mije.com	Hostel, all-ages welcome, well-located, clean dorm rooms, prices per person
$ MIJE Maubisson 12 Rue des Barres tel. 01 42 74 23 45 mije.com	Small, quiet hostel with same rates as MIJE Fourcy
$$ Hôtel de la Bretonnerie*** 22 Rue Ste. Croix de la Bretonnerie tel. 01 48 87 77 63 bretonnerie.com	Warm lobby, well-appointed, good-value rooms with character, no A/C
$$ Hôtel Beaubourg*** 11 Rue Simon Le Franc tel. 01 42 74 34 24 beaubourg-paris-hotel.com	Terrific value on a quiet street in the shadow of the Pompidou Center
$$ Hôtel de Nice** 42 bis Rue de Rivoli tel. 01 42 78 55 29 hoteldenice.com	On busy road; colorful decor, thoughtful touches, and tight bathrooms
$ Hôtel du Loiret* 8 Rue des Mauvais Garçons tel. 01 48 87 77 00 hotel-du-loiret.fr	Rare Marais budget hotel, noisy but sharp rooms, no A/C

ILE ST. LOUIS AREA—Island in the Seine near Notre-Dame; peaceful, residential, and pricey; Metro stops Pont Marie and Sully-Morland	
$$$ Hôtel du Jeu de Paume** 54 Rue St Louis en-l'Ile tel. 01 43 26 14 18 jeudepaumehotel.com	Wonderful location, magnificent place with half-timbered lobby and plush rooms
$$$ Hôtel de Lutèce* 65 Rue St. Louis-en-l'Ile tel. 01 43 26 23 52 paris-hotel-lutece.com	Cozy lobby with a real fireplace, warmly appointed rooms
$$$ Hôtel des Deux-Iles* 59 Rue St. Louis-en-l'Ile tel. 01 43 26 13 35 deuxiles-paris-hotel.com	Bright and colorful, with small but well-configured rooms
LUXEMBOURG GARDEN AREA—Left Bank energy with shops, cafés, and the park; Metro stops St. Sulpice, Rennes, Sèvres-Babylone, Mabillon, Odéon, and St. Germain-des-Prés	
$$$ Hôtel le Récamier** 3 bis Place St. Sulpice tel. 01 43 26 04 89 hotelrecamier.com	Boutique hotel on Place St. Sulpice, snazzy rooms and public spaces
$$$ Hôtel de l'Abbaye** 10 Rue Cassette tel. 01 45 44 38 11 hotelabbayeparis.com	Refuge with sumptuous rooms and public spaces, includes breakfast
$$ Hôtel Bonaparte* 61 Rue Bonaparte tel. 01 43 26 97 37 hotelbonaparte.fr	Unpretentious, welcoming place with Old World rooms at good prices
$ Hôtel Jean Bart** 9 Rue Jean-Bart tel. 01 45 48 29 13 hotel.jean.bart@gmail.com	Basic hotel near Luxembourg Garden, no A/C, cash only

$$$ Hôtel Relais Médicis*** 23 Rue Racine tel. 01 43 26 00 60 relaismedicis.com	Refuge with Old World charm near Odéon Theater, includes breakfast
$$ Hôtel des Grandes Ecoles*** 75 Rue du Cardinal Lemoine tel. 01 43 26 79 23 hotel-grandes-ecoles.com	Lovely rooms around a peaceful, flowery courtyard, no A/C
$ Hôtel des 3 Collèges** 16 Rue Cujas tel. 01 43 54 67 30 3colleges.com	Bright lobby, narrow hallways, and unimaginative rooms, fair rates
$ Hôtel Cujas Panthéon** 18 Rue Cujas tel. 01 43 54 58 10 cujas-pantheon-paris-hotel.com	Traditional comfort at fair prices
$ Hôtel Cluny Sorbonne** 8 Rue Victor Cousin tel. 01 43 54 66 66 hotel-cluny.fr	Modest, warmly run place across from the Sorbonne, thin walls, no A/C
$$ Hôtel des Mines** 125 Boulevard St. Michel tel. 01 43 54 32 78 hoteldesminesparis.com	Less central but a good value, comfortable rooms at fair prices

BOTTOM OF RUE MOUFFETARD—Blue-collar by day, bohemian at night; not so central, but a good value; Metro stops Censier-Daubenton and Les Gobelins

$ Port-Royal-Hôtel* 8 Boulevard de Port-Royal tel. 01 43 31 70 06 hotelportroyal.fr	Immaculate hotel on busy street with comfortable rooms, cash only
$ Hôtel de L'Espérance** 15 Rue Pascal tel. 01 47 07 10 99 hoteldelesperance.fr	Terrific value with quiet, cushy rooms, and pleasing public spaces

$ Young & Happy Hostel 80 Rue Mouffetard tel. 01 47 07 47 07 youngandhappy.fr	Easygoing hostel with kitchen facilities, acceptable conditions, no A/C, rates per person

MONTMARTRE AREA—Lively, un-touristy base of the hill, great for young and budget travelers; Metro stops Abbesses and Anvers

$ Hôtel Regyn's** 18 Place des Abbesses tel. 01 42 54 45 21 hotel-regyns-paris.com	Small, comfortable rooms with mediocre bathrooms at good rates, no A/C
$ My Hôtel in France Montmartre 57 Rue des Abbesses tel. 01 42 51 50 00 myhotelinfrance-montmartre.com	Basic hotel with well-maintained rooms, free breakfast, no A/C, no elevator
$ Plug-Inn Boutique Hostel 7 Rue Aristide Bruant tel. 01 42 58 42 58 plug-inn.fr	Hostel-like hotel, free breakfast, kitchen facilities, rates per person
$ Hôtel Bonséjour Montmartre 11 Rue Burq tel. 01 42 54 22 53 hotel-bonsejour-montmartre.fr	Old, worn place with shared bathrooms, and dirt-cheap prices, no A/C, no elevator

Sleeping

Eating

The Parisian eating scene is kept at a rolling boil. Entire books (and lives) are dedicated to the subject, and trendy chefs are stalked by the *paparazzi*. Parisians eat long and well. Relaxed lunches, three-hour dinners, and endless hours of sitting in outdoor cafés are the norm. Budget some money—and time—to sightseeing for your palate. Even if the rest of you is sleeping in a cheap hotel, let your taste buds travel first-class in Paris.

I list a full range of restaurants and eateries, from budget options for a quick bite to multi-course splurges with maximum ambience. My listings are in Paris' atmospheric neighborhoods, handy to recommended hotels and sights.

Restaurant Price Code

$$$ Most main courses €25 or more
$$ Most main courses €15-25.
$ Most main courses €15 or less.

Based on the average price of a meat or seafood dish on the menu. Salads and appetizers are several euros cheaper. So a typical meal at a $$ restaurant—including appetizer, main dish, house wine, water, and service—would cost about €40.

When in Paris...

When in Paris, I eat on the Parisian schedule. For breakfast, I eat at the hotel or belly up to a café counter for a quick *café au lait* and croissant. Lunch (12:00-14:00) may be a big salad or *plat du jour,* or an atmospheric picnic. In the late afternoon, Parisians enjoy a beverage at a sidewalk table. Dinner is the time for slowing down and savoring a multi-course restaurant meal.

Restaurants

Restaurants and bistros start serving dinner to tourists around 19:00, to locals after 20:00, and can be packed by 21:00. Many restaurants close Sunday and Monday. All café and restaurant interiors are smoke-free, but outdoor tables can be smoky.

A full restaurant meal comes in courses. It might include an *apéritif* (before-dinner drink), an *entrée* (appetizer), a *plat* (main dish), cheese course, dessert, coffee, liqueurs, several different wines, and so on.

It's not obligatory to order every course—in fact, many Parisians these days consider two courses (e.g., *plat* and dessert) a "full" meal. Ordering as little as a single main dish as your entire meal is acceptable. Couples could each order a *plat* and share a starter or dessert. If you want to eat lighter than that, try a café or brasserie instead. Since even a two- or three-course restaurant meal can take hours, and the costs can add up quickly, plan your strategy before sitting down to a full meal.

Most restaurants offer a good-value *"menu"* or *"formule"*—a multi-course meal at a fixed price where you can choose from a list of select items. In addition, many places serve a daily special *plat du jour* (a main dish plus a side, on a single plate), though it may only be offered at lunch.

Parisians are willing to pay for bottled water with their meal *(eau minérale),* but a free carafe of tap water *(une carafe d'eau)* is always available upon request, and more bread is also free.

The service charge is automatically built into your bill's total, so there's no need to tip. For exceptional service, you could tip up to 5 percent, though Parisians rarely do. Waiters probably won't overwhelm you with friendliness or attention—it's not the French style.

To get the most out of your Parisian restaurant—slow down. Allow ample time for the meal, engage the waiter, show you're serious about food, consider his or her recommendations, and enjoy the experience as much as the food itself.

Here's a typical restaurant experience: To get the waiter's attention, simply ask, *"S'il vous plaît?"* He or she will bring a menu *(carte)* and ask what you'd like to drink *(Vous voulez quelque choses à boire?).* He'll return with the drinks and ask if you're ready to order *(Vous êtes prêts à commander?).* Then he'll bring your meal—*"Bon appétit."* When he comes to clear your plates, he'll ask if you're finished *(Vous avez terminé?),* and if you'd like dessert or coffee. If you're in any kind of hurry, this is the time to also ask for the bill—*L'addition, s'il vous plaît.* If you don't ask, they won't bring it automatically: That would be considered rude.

Cafés and Brasseries

Less formal than restaurants, these places serve user friendly meals, as well as coffee and drinks. They serve food throughout the day, and you're welcome to order just a single dish (even for dinner), rather than a multi-course meal.

Feel free to order a *plat* (main course), a *plat du jour* (daily special), a salad (they're usually big), a sandwich (e.g. a *croque monsieur,* or grilled ham and cheese sandwich), an omelet, an *entrée* (appetizer), or a bowl of soup. It's also fine to split starters and desserts, though not main courses. Many cafés and brasseries have outdoor tables (with braziers in winter) perfect for nursing a glass of wine or cafe au lait, and watching the parade of passersbys. A crêperie—serving both sweet dessert crepes and meal-like savory ones—is another less formal, budget alternative.

Be aware that the price of drinks may be 20-40 percent more if you consume them while sitting at a table *(salle)* instead of standing at the bar *(comptoir).* Outdoor tables can sometimes be more expensive still. The prices will always be clearly posted. Don't sit without first checking out the financial consequences.

Picnicking

Paris makes it easy to turn a picnic into a first-class affair. Take-out delis (a *charcuterie* or *traiteur,* as well as some bakeries) sell high-quality cooked dishes, quiches, pâtés, small pizzas, and salads you can build a meal around. The deli can warm it up for you *(chauffé* = heated up) and pack it in a take-out box *(une barquette),* along with a plastic fork *(fourchette).*

For side dishes, a generic *supermarché* is easy for one-stop shopping, but you'll do better browsing a *boulangerie* for your baguette, a *fromagerie* for cheese, and an open-air market for the freshest produce.

Be daring. Try the smelly cheeses, ugly pâtés, and sissy quiches. Some good picnic spots in the heart of Paris are the Palais Royal courtyard, the Place des Vosges, the west tip of Ile de la Cité, and the Tuileries Garden.

Parisian Cuisine

There is no "Parisian cuisine" to speak of. Rather, Paris is France's melting pot. You'll find dishes from every French region, and many restaurants specialize in a particular regional cuisine.

From Burgundy (among France's best cuisines), try *coq au vin* (chicken with wine sauce), *bœuf bourguignon* (beef stew), or *escargots.* From Normandy and Brittany you'll find mussels and oysters, crepes, and cider. Any dish prepared *à la provençale* features that region's garlic, olive oil, herbs, and tomatoes. You'll find *bouillabaisse* from the Côte d'Azur, *pâté de foie gras* (goose-liver pâté) from the southwest, and even Alsatian *choucroute*—sauerkraut.

Paris has a particular fondness for steak, including steak tartare—raw ground beef. Duck from the southwest *(confit de canard),* leg of lamb *(gigot d'agneau),* roasted chicken *(poulet roti),* and salmon *(saumon)* are also popular. Raw oysters *(huîtres)* from Brittany are a Christmas tradition. Sauces are a huge part of French cooking. The five classics are *béchamel* (milk-based white sauce), *espagnole* (veal-based brown sauce), *velouté* (stock-based white sauce), *tomate* (tomato-based red sauce), and *hollandaise* (egg yolk-based white sauce).

Commonly served cheeses are Brie de Meaux (mild and creamy, from just outside Paris), Camembert (semicreamy and pungent, from Normandy), *chèvre* (goat cheese from the Loire), and Roquefort (strong and blue-veined, from south-central France). Many restaurants will bring you a variety platter you can choose from.

For dessert, try a *café gourmand,* an assortment of small desserts selected by the restaurant. Other classic desserts include crème bruleé, *tarte-tatin,* and *mousse au chocolat.*

No meal in France is complete without wine. Even the basic house wine *(vin ordinaire,* or *vin du maison)* is fine with a meal—order it by the pitcher, or *pichet.* For good-but-inexpensive wines by the bottle, look for reds from Côtes du Rhone or Languedoc, and whites from Burgundy or Alsace. In summer, everyone should try an inexpensive rosé. Those willing to pay more can get a good (but not cheap) pinot noir from Burgundy, or a heavier red from Bordeaux.

The French do not drink wine as *apéritifs.* More common are champagne, beer, a Kir (a dash of crème de Cassis with white wine) or Pastis (an anise-flavored liquor from Provence). France's best beer is Alsatian; try Kronenbourg or the heavier Pelfort. *Une panaché* is a refreshing French shandy (7-Up and beer).

For coffee, Parisians like *une café* (shot of espresso), a *café au lait* (coffee plus steamed milk, aka *un café creme),* or *une noisette* (espresso with a shot of milk). A fun, bright, nonalcoholic drink is *un diablo menthe,* featuring 7-Up with mint syrup. If you're ordering a Coke, remember that Paris' last ice cubes melted after the last Yankee tour group left.

Eating

RUE CLER AREA—Eateries catering to upscale residents near the Eiffel Tower (see map, pages 192-193)

❶	**$ Café du Marché** 38 Rue Cler tel. 01 47 05 51 27	High-energy, great outdoor seating right on Rue Cler (Mon-Sat 11:00-23:00, Sun 11:00-17:00)
❷	**$ Tribeca Italian Restaurant** Located next to Café du Marché	Same owners as Café du Marché, with Italian theme (open daily)
❸	**$ Le Petit Cler** 29 Rue Cler tel. 01 45 50 17 50	Tiny, traditional café with leather booths, fine food, and a few outdoor tables (closed Mon)
❹	**$ Crêperie Ulysée en Gaule** 28 Rue Cler, tel. 01 47 05 61 82	Cheapest seats on Rue Cler with crêpes to go (open daily)
❺	**$$ Le Florimond** 19 Avenue de la Motte-Picquet tel. 01 45 55 40 38	Intimate and welcoming, with classic French cuisine, reservations smart (closed Sun)
❻	**$$ Au Petit Tonneau** 20 Rue Surcouf tel. 01 47 05 09 01	Small bistro with real-deal ambience, limited but good selections (closed Mon)
❼	**$$ Café le Bosquet** 46 Avenue Bosquet tel. 01 45 51 38 13	Modern brasserie with dressy waiters, sit inside or out, good-value menu (closed Sun)
❽	**$$ La Terrasse du 7ème** 2 Place de L'Ecole Militaire tel. 01 45 55 00 02	Busy café with grand outdoor seating and a living-room interior (open daily until 24:00, sometimes later)
❾	**$$ Le Petit Niçois** 10 Rue Amélie tel. 01 45 51 83 65	Delicious seafood at fair prices—try the *marmite du pêcheur* (open daily)
❿	**$$ Au Petit Sud Ouest** 46 Avenue de la Bourdonnais tel. 01 45 55 59 59	Wood-beam coziness for southwestern specialties: foie gras, cassoulet, duck (closed Sun-Mon)
⓫	**$$$ 58 Tour Eiffel** Mo: Bir-Hakeim tel. 08 25 56 66 62	Snazzy place in the Eiffel Tower (first floor), reserve way ahead for view tables (open daily)
⓬	**$$ Le P'tit Troquet** 28 Rue de l'Exposition tel. 01 47 05 80 39	Soft, intimate, and welcoming bistro with fragile elegance and wonderful meals (opens at 18:00, closed Sun)

⑬	**$$ Café Constant** 139 Rue St. Dominique tel. 01 47 53 73 34	Cool, two-level place with delicious and affordable dishes
⑭	**$$$ Le Violon d'Ingres** 135 Rue St. Dominique tel. 01 45 55 15 05	Chef Christian Constant serves top cuisine in a modern setting, reservations essential (open daily)
⑮	**$ Boulangerie-Pâtisserie de la Tour Eiffel** 21 Avenue de la Bourdonnais tel. 01 47 05 59 81	Inexpensive salads, quiches, sandwiches, and Eiffel Tower views (open daily)
⑯	**$ La Varangue** 27 Rue Augereau tel. 01 47 05 51 22	Friendly, entertaining one-man show with simple and cheap meals (closed Sun)

MARAIS AREA—Trendy places amid boisterous nightlife (see map, pages 194–195)

⑰	**$$$ Ma Bourgogne** 19 Place des Vosges tel. 01 42 78 44 64	Vintage eatery on Place des Vosges, serving French specialties (open daily)
⑱	**$$ Café Hugo** 22 Place des Vosges tel. 01 42 72 04 04	Terrific setting, basic café fare, best for drinks only (open daily)
⑲	**$$ La Place Royale** 2 bis Place des Vosges tel. 01 42 78 58 16	On the square, warm welcome, good-value wines and menus (open daily, all day)
⑳	**$$ Les Bonnes Soeurs** 8 Rue du pas de la Mule tel. 01 42 74 55 80	Blends modern and traditional fare with contemporary ambience and big portions (open daily)
㉑	**$$ Brasserie Bofinger** 5 Rue de la Bastille tel. 01 42 72 87 82	Vintage, sprawling place famous for fish and traditional, with Alsatian flair (open daily)
㉒	**$$ Chez Janou** 2 Rue Roger Verlomme tel. 01 42 72 28 41	Lively Provençal bistro with Mediterranean cuisine, sit inside or out (open daily from 19:45)
㉓	**$$ Robert et Louise** 64 Rue du Vieille du Temple tel. 01 42 78 55 89	Cramped rustic-as-it-gets interior, food is red-meat good, well-priced (closed Mon)

Eating

㉔	**$$ Au Temps des Cerises** 31 Rue de la Cerisaie tel. 01 42 72 08 63	Local wine bar with 1950s atmosphere, tight seating, and character (open daily)
㉕	**$ Le Bistrot des Compères** 16 Rue Charlemagne tel. 01 42 72 14 16	On quiet corner in thick of Marais, welcoming feel, sit inside or out (closed Sun-Mon)
㉖	**$ Le Marché** and **Au Bistrot de la Place** Place du Marché Ste. Catherine	Two fun, cheap places on the Marais' most romantic and charming square (both open daily)
㉗	**$ Breizh (Brittany) Café** 109 Rue du Vieille du Temple tel. 01 42 72 13 77	Simple Breton place with delicious organic crêpes, sparkling cider (12:00 to late, closed Mon-Tue)
㉘	**$ Chez Marianne** 2 Rue des Hospitalières-St.-Gervais, tel. 01 42 72 18 86	Blends delicious Jewish cuisine with Parisian élan in a cluttered wine shop (open long hours daily)
㉙	**$ Le Loir dans la Théière** 3 Rue des Rosiers tel. 01 42 72 90 61	Cozy teahouse for baked goods, hot drinks, and weekend brunch (Mon-Fri 12:00-19:00, Sat-Sun 10:00-19:00)
㉚	**$ L'As du Falafel** 34 Rue des Rosiers tel. 01 48 87 63 60	Best falafel in the Jewish Quarter, as well as other tasty dishes (long hours, closed Fri eve and Sat)
㉛	**$$ Au Bourguignon du Marais** 52 Rue Francois Miron tel. 01 48 87 15 40	Handsome wine-bar/bistro with fine cuisine, ideal for Burgundy-lovers (closed Sun-Mon)
㉜	**$ L'Ebouillanté** 6 Rue des Barres tel. 01 42 71 09 69	Breezy, romantic crêperie-café (open daily 12:00-21:30, closed Mon in winter)

ILE ST. LOUIS—Quiet, romantic area perfect for after-dinner strolling (see map, pages 192-193)

㉝	**$$$ Le Tastevin** 46 Rue St. Louis-en-l'Ile tel. 01 43 54 17 31	Intimate restaurant serving fine meals in a romantic setting under wooden beams (open daily)
㉞	**$$$ Nos Ancêtres les Gaulois** 39 Rue St. Louis-en-l'Ile tel. 01 46 33 66 07	All you can eat and drink for €41 in a rowdy, medieval cellar (daily from 19:00)

㉟	**$$ Brasserie de l'Ile St. Louis** 55 Quai de Bourbon tel. 01 40 54 02 50	Purely Alsatian cuisine served in a vigorous, Teutonic setting (closed Wed)
㊱	**$ L'Orangerie** 28 Rue St. Louis-en-l'Ile tel. 01 46 33 93 98	Inviting place with soft lighting, comfortable seating, and delicious cuisine (closed Mon)
㊲	**$ Auberge de la Reine Blanche** 30 Rue St. Louis-en-l'Ile tel. 01 46 33 07 87	Tasty cuisine at unbeatable prices in a cozy setting (daily from 18:00)
㊳	**$ Café Med** 77 Rue St. Louis-en-l'Ile tel. 01 43 29 73 17	Inexpensive salads, crêpes, and plats in a tight but cheery setting (open daily)

LUXEMBOURG GARDEN AREA—Lively near St. Sulpice, quieter near Panthéon (see map, pages 192-193)

㊴	**$ La Crêpe Rit du Clown** 6 Rue des Canettes tel. 01 46 34 01 02	Yummy crêpes on a fun, traffic-free street (Mon-Sat 12:00-23:00, closed Sun)
㊵	**$$ Lou Pescadou-Chez Julien** 16 Rue Mabillon, tel. 01 43 54 56 08	Good bistro fare in an intimate, appealing setting (open daily)
㊶	**$ Santa Lucia** 22 Rue des Canettes tel. 01 43 26 42 68	Wood-fired pizza, good pasta, and killer tiramisu (closed Mon)
㊷	**$$ Les Deux Magots** and **Le Café de Flore** Place St. Germain-des-Prés	Two famous cafés on a famous boulevard with a famous clientele (open daily)
㊸	**$$ La Méditerranée** 2 Place de l'Odéon tel. 01 43 26 02 30	Gourmet Mediterranean in lovely setting, Odéon view, reservations smart (open daily)
㊹	**$ Restaurant Polidor** 41 Rue Monsieur-le-Prince tel. 01 43 26 95 34	Bare-bones bistro with unpretentious cooking and fun old-Paris atmosphere (open daily)
㊺	**$$ Le Vin Qui Danse** 4 Rue des Fossés Saint-Jacques tel. 01 43 54 80 81	Warm little place serving tasty dishes and well-matched wines (open daily)
㊻	**$ Le Soufflot Café** 16 Rue Soufflot tel. 01 43 26 57 56	Library-like interior and great outside seating with brilliant Panthéon views (open daily)

Eating

Rue Cler Area Restaurants

To Pont
de l'Alma

RUE DE MONTTESSUY

RUE VALENTIN

AVENUE RAPP

AVENUE BOSQUET

PASSAGE LANDRIEU

RUE LOGES

15
B #42

B #42
← To Eiffel
Tower & **11**

AVE. DE LA BOURDONNAIS

7e

RUE ST-DOMINIQUE

B #80 &
#92

B #69

B #80 &
#92

AVE. ELISEE RECLUS

← To Eiffel
Tower & **11**

T

13 **14**

RUE DE LA EXPOSITION

RUE AUGEREAU

RUE JOSEPH BOUVARD

B #42, #69
& #87

10

12

#69

B #80 &
#92

RUE DE GRENELLE

T B

B #80 &
#92

AVENUE BOSQUET

B #69 &
#87

16

P

#87 B

Place
Jacques
Rueff

B #69

7

B #69

Parc du
Champ de Mars

ALLEE ADRIENNE LECOUVREUR

#87 B

AVE. DE LA BOURDONNAIS

KIDS' PLAY
AREA &
PUPPETS

AVE. EMILE DESCHANEL

#28, #80 B
& #92

KIDS' PLAYGROUND

RUE MALAR

RUE JEAN NICOT

5 min. walk to
Seine River &
American Church

R. SURCOUF

Ⓑ #28

Ⓑ 6

Ⓣ

RUE ST-DOMINIQUE

BLVD. DE LA-TOUR-MAUBOURG

Ⓑ
#69

ST.
PIERRE

Ⓑ #69

RUE FABERT

Place des
Invalides

PASSAGE J. NICOT

RUE DE LA COMÈTE

Ⓑ 9

RUE AMÉLIE

To Rodin
Museum

#69
Ⓑ

Ⓑ #69

RUE DE GRENELLE

Ⓣ

Ⓜ

La Tour-
Maubourg

RUE JUVISIER

RUE PSICHARI

ST.
JEAN

VALADON

Ⓑ 4   Ⓑ 3

Ⓑ 2

Ⓑ 1

RUE CLER

RUE DU CHAMP DE MARS

RUE
CLER

AVE. DE LA MOTTE-PICQUET

RUE CHEVERT

ARMY
MUSEUM &
NAPOLEON'S
TOMB

POST ◆

Ⓑ 5

7e

Ⓑ 8

MUSEUM
ENTRANCE

Ⓜ

Ecole
Militaire

Ⓜ

Place de
l'Ecole
Militaire

Ecole
Militaire

#87 &
#92

Ⓑ Ⓣ

To Rodin
Museum

Ⓑ #92

AVE. DE TOURVILLE

Ⓑ #92

ECOLE
MILITAIRE

#87 Ⓑ

A. DUQUESNE

Ⓑ #92

Place
Vauban

Marais, Ile St. Louis & Luxembourg Garden Restaurants

Eating

GARE DU NORD

Practicalities

PLANNING

Paris' best travel months—also the busiest and most expensive for flights and hotels—are May, June, September, and October. The summer heat in July and August can be unpleasant (though hotel rates can drop). Paris makes a great winter getaway. Although it's cold and rainy, crowds are less, cafés are cozy, and the city feels lively but not touristy.

Make sure your passport is up to date (to renew, see travel.state .gov). Call your debit- and credit-card companies about your plans. Book hotel rooms well in advance, especially for peak season (May, June, Sept, Oct) and holidays. Consider buying travel insurance. Book an entrance time at the Eiffel Tower, to avoid long lines. If you're traveling beyond Paris, research railpasses, TGV train reservations, and car rentals.

MONEY

France uses the euro currency: 1 euro (€1) = about $1.30. To convert euros to dollars add about 30 percent: €20 = about $26, €50 = about $65. (Check oanda.com for the latest exchange rates.)

Withdraw money from an ATM (known as a *distributeur* in France) using a debit card, just like at home. Visa and MasterCard are commonly used throughout Europe. Before departing, call your bank or credit-card company: Ask about international transaction fees, and alert them that you'll be making withdrawals in Europe. Many travelers bring a second debit or credit card as a backup.

While American magnetic-stripe credit cards are accepted almost everywhere in Europe, they may not work in some automated payment machines geared for European-style chip-and-PIN cards (e.g., buying Métro tickets from a machine). Be prepared to pay with cash, try entering your card's PIN, or find a nearby cashier.

To keep your valuables safe, wear a money belt. But if you do lose your credit or debit card, report the loss immediately with a phone call: Visa (tel. 08 00 90 11 79), MasterCard (tel. 08 00 90 13 87), and American Express (tel. 01 47 77 70 00).

Helpful Websites

Paris' Tourist Information: parisinfo.com
France's Tourist Information: franceguide.com.
Passports and Red Tape: travel.state.gov
Cheap Flights: kayak.com (for international flights), skyscanner.com (for flights within Europe)
Airplane Carry-on Restrictions: tsa.gov
General Info on Paris Topics: bonjourparis.com or paris-anglo.com
European Train Schedules: bahn.com
General Travel Tips: ricksteves.com (helpful info on train travel, railpasses, car rental, travel insurance, packing lists, and much more—plus updates to this book)

ARRIVAL IN PARIS

Charles de Gaulle Airport

Paris' main airport has three terminals: T-1, T-2, and T-3. All have ATMs, banks, shops, and bars. There are tourist information offices in T-1 (arrivals hall, door 6) and T-2, as well as helpful orange ADP info desks. You can travel between terminals on the free CDGVAL automated shuttle train or on free shuttle buses (allow 30 minutes). For airport information, call 3950 or visit adp.fr (airport code: CDG).

To get between any of the airport's three terminals and downtown Paris, you have several options:

Taxi: The one-hour trip costs about €65 for up to four people with bags (fourth passenger costs €3 extra). For trips from Paris to the airport, have your hotel arrange it a day in advance.

Roissy-Bus: Buses make the 50-minute trip to the Opéra Métro stop in central Paris, arriving on Rue Scribe (€10, 3-4/hour, runs 6:00-23:00, buy ticket on bus). From there, it's an easy Métro ride to anywhere in the city.

"Les Cars" Air France Bus: Bus #2 goes to Etoile/Arc de Triomphe and Porte Maillot (45 minutes). Bus #4 runs to Gare de Lyon (45 minutes) and the Montparnasse Tower/train station (€16.50, at least 2/hour, runs

5:45-23:00, toll tel. 08 92 35 08 20, lescarsairfrance.com). All stops are on Métro lines.

RER-B Trains: This option is cheaper but more complicated. Follow *Paris by Train* signs, then *RER* signs. The train serves Gare du Nord, Châtelet-Les Halles, St. Michel, and Luxembourg (€9.60, 4/hour, runs 5:00-24:00, 30 minutes to Gare du Nord).

Airport Vans: These shuttle vans work like those at home, carrying passengers directly to or from their hotels, with stops along the way to pick up other passengers. They cost about €32 for one person, €46 for two, or €58 for three. Ask your hotel to arrange one or try Paris Shuttles Network (tel. 01 45 26 01 58, shuttlesnetwork.com), Airport Connection (tel. 01 43 65 55 55, supershuttle.fr), or the higher-priced but intensive-service Paris Webservices (pariswebservices.com).

Other Arrival Points

Orly Airport: Paris' second airport is smaller, but its two terminals—Ouest (west) and Sud (south)—have all the conveniences. Helpful orange ADP information desks are near baggage claim. For flight info call 3950, or visit adp.fr (airport code: ORY). To get into Paris, you can take a taxi (€45); or catch the "Les Cars" Air France bus to Gare Montparnasse, Invalides (near Rue Cler), or Etoile (€12, buy ticket from driver, 4/hour, 40 minutes); or ask at the airport TI for other options.

Paris' Train Stations: Paris has six major stations, each serving different regions. For example, to go to London on the Eurostar, you leave from Gare du Nord. Trains to Chartres leave from Gare Montparnasse. The best all-Europe train schedule information is online at bahn.com. The French national rail website is sncf.com. Book TGV trains well in advance at tgv-europe.com. To see if a railpass could save you money, check rick steves.com/rail.

HELPFUL HINTS

Tourist Information (TI): Don't go out of your way tracking down Paris' official TIs, which often have long lines. But if you do come across one (e.g., at Charles de Gaulle airport), pick up a free map and a "Paris for You" brochure, and consider buying a Museum Pass (parisinfo.com).

Bookstores: English-language bookstores include the venerable

Tipping

Tipping in France isn't as generous as it is in the US. To tip a taxi driver, round up to the next euro on the fare (for a €4.50 fare, give €5). For longer rides, figure about 10 percent. At hotels, if you let the porter carry your luggage, tip a euro for each bag. If you like to tip maids, leave a euro per night at the end of your stay.

For sit-down service in a restaurant, a 12-15 percent service charge is always already included in the list price of the food *(service compris)*. Most Parisians never tip. However, if you feel the service was *exceptional*, it's fine to tip up to 5 percent extra. When you hand your payment plus a tip to your waiter, you can say, *"C'est bon"* (say bohn), meaning, "It's good."

Shakespeare and Company (near Notre-Dame, 37 Rue de la Bûcherie, tel. 01 43 25 40 93); W. H. Smith alongside the Tuileries Garden (248 Rue de Rivoli, Mo: Concorde, tel. 01 44 77 88 99); and the San Francisco Book Company near Luxembourg Garden (17 Rue Monsieur le Prince, Mo: Odéon, tel. 01 43 29 15 70)

Hurdling the Language Barrier: Most Parisians speak some English—certainly more English than Americans speak French. Still, learn the pleasantries like *bonjour* (good day), *pardon* (pardon me), *s'il vous plaît* (please), *merci* (thank you), and *au revoir* (goodbye). Begin every encounter with *"Bonjour, Madame* or *Monsieur,"* or *"s'il vous plaît,"* and ask *"Parlez-vous anglais?"* End every encounter with *"Au revoir, Madame* or *Monsieur."* For more French survival phrases, ✪ see page 217.

Time: France's time zone is six/nine hours ahead of the East/West Coasts of the US.

Business Hours: Most businesses are open Monday through Saturday, roughly 10:00-19:00. Smaller shops may close for lunch (12:00-14:00) and on Monday mornings until 14:00. Banks close on Saturday. On Sunday morning, some small markets, *boulangeries* (bakeries), and street markets are open until noon. Handy hole-in-the-wall grocery stores stay open every day until midnight.

Watt's Up? Europe's electrical system is 220 volts, instead of North America's 110 volts. You'll need an adapter plug with two round prongs, sold inexpensively at travel stores in the US. Most newer electronics convert automatically, so you won't need a separate converter.

Laundry: Paris has no shortage of self-serve launderettes, charging about €8 to wash and dry a load—ask your hotelier for the closest one.

Pedestrian Safety: Parisian drivers are notorious for ignoring pedestrians. Look both ways. Don't assume you have the right of way, even in a crosswalk. Be aware that many streets are one-way, and be careful of seemingly quiet bus/taxi lanes. Bicycles are silent but dangerous, lurking in the bus/taxi lane or going the wrong way on a one-way street.

WCs: Paris has some free public toilets (tipping the attendant is appropriate) and some coin-op "toilet-booths" along the sidewalks. Otherwise, use restrooms in museums, or walk into any sidewalk café like you own the place, and find the toilet in the back.

Tabacs: These handy little neighborhood shops sell phone cards, postage stamps, Métro tickets, sometimes Museum Passes, and...oh yeah, cigarettes. They're a slice of workaday Paris.

GETTING AROUND PARIS

In Paris, you're never more than a 10-minute walk from a Métro station, and buses are everywhere. Study the fold-out Métro map at the back of this book, buy a *carnet* of 10 tickets, learn a few handy bus lines, and Paris is yours. For more information on Paris' public transportation system, visit ratp.fr.

Buying Tickets

The same ticket works on the Métro, RER suburban trains (within the city), and city buses. A single ticket costs €1.70 and is valid for as many transfers as you need to make a single journey within 90 minutes (but not to transfer between Métro/RER and bus).

To save money, buy a *carnet* of 10 tickets for €13.30. Or you could consider the one-day Mobilis pass (€6.60) or the weekly Passe Navigo, a chip-embedded card (€19.80 plus €5 first-time fee and €5 for ID photo). Which is best? It's hard to beat the *carnet*. Two 10-packs of *carnets*—enough for most travelers staying a week—cost about €27 and can be shared between travel partners. The Passe Navigo only becomes worthwhile for visitors who stay a full week (beginning on a Monday) and use the system a lot.

Buy tickets and passes at most Métro stations or at some *tabac* shops. Be aware that not every Métro station has a staffed ticket window (where you can buy tickets using cash or American-style magnetic-stripe credit cards). However, all stations have ticket-vending machines that accept coins (and chip-and-PIN credit cards, which few Americans have).

By Métro

Europe's best underground train system runs daily 5:30-24:30, Fri-Sat until 2:00 in the morning. Begin by studying a Métro map.

Find the Métro stop closest to you and the stop closest to your destination. Next see which lines connect those two points. The lines are color-coded and numbered, and are known by their end-of-the-line stops.

In the Métro station, signs direct you to the train line going in your direction (e.g., *direction: La Défense*). Insert your ticket in the turnstile, reclaim it, pass through, and hang onto your ticket until you exit the system. To make transfers, follow orange *correspondance* (connection) signs. Be prepared to walk significant distances within Métro stations. Once you reach your final stop, look for the blue-and-white *sortie* (exit) signs. Use the helpful neighborhood maps to choose the *sortie* closest to where you want to go. After you exit the system, toss or tear your used ticket so you don't confuse it with unused tickets.

Be wary of thieves in the Métro—while you're preoccupied buying tickets, passing through turnstiles, and contending with the jostle of boarding and leaving crowded trains.

By RER: The RER suburban train line works just like the Métro and uses the same ticket (valid within the city center only; transfers OK between Métro and RER). On your Métro map, the RER routes are the thick lines labeled A, B, C, and so on. Many trains don't stop at every station—check the sign over the platform to see if your destination is listed as a stop.

By City Bus

Paris' excellent bus system works like buses anywhere. Every bus stop has a name, and every bus is headed to one end-of-the-line stop or the other. One bus/Métro/RER ticket gets you anywhere in central Paris within the freeway ring road. It's good for transfers between buses within 90 minutes, but not from bus to Métro/RER, or for multiple trips on the same bus line.

Board your bus through the front door. Validate your ticket or scan your Passe Navigo. Push the red button to signal the driver you want a stop, then exit through the rear door. Avoid rush hour—Monday-Friday 8:00-9:30 & 17:30-19:30—when the Métro is a better option.

Bus #69 runs east-west between the Eiffel Tower and Père Lachaise Cemetery by way of the Rue Cler, Orsay Museum, Louvre, and the Marais. Scenic bus #73 runs from the Orsay Museum up the Champs-Elysées to the Arc de Triomphe. I always check the bus stop near my hotel to see if it's convenient to my plans.

By Taxi

Parisian taxis are reasonable, especially for couples and families, who can split the cost. Fares and supplements (described in English on the rear windows) are straightforward and regulated. A taxi can fit three people comfortably, and a fourth for €3 extra.

The meter starts at €2.50, and there's a minimum total of €6.50. A typical 20-minute ride (e.g., Place Bastille to Eiffel Tower) costs about €20. Taxis can charge higher rates at rush hour, at night, all day Sunday, to airports, and €1 for each piece of luggage you put in the trunk. To tip, round up to the next euro, or (for longer rides) about 10 percent.

You can try waving down a taxi, or find the nearest taxi stand—they're marked with a ⓣ on this book's maps. To order a taxi, call 01 41 27 66 99 (or ask your hotelier); the meter starts running as soon as the call is received, adding about €6 to the bill. Taxis are tough to find during rush hour, when it's raining, and on Friday and Saturday nights. If you need to catch an early morning train or flight, book your taxi at least the day before; your hotel can help.

By Bike

Paris is great by bicycle. The city is flat, there are more than 370 miles of bike and bus-priority lanes, and Parisian drivers are growing accustomed to sharing the road.

Rental bikes are everywhere, thanks to the city-wide Vélib' program. Locals can just swipe a card at one of 1,500 stations, take a bike off the rack, and return it at any station when they're done. While the stations require payment with a European-style chip-and-PIN credit card, you can get around this restriction by booking a short-term subscription in advance online: Go to en.velib.paris.fr, click "Subscription and Fees," then scroll down and choose the "Short-Term Subscription" that works for you.

You can rent bikes from Bike About Tours near Hôtel de Ville (€15/day, 4 Rue de Lobau in Vinci parking garage, bikeabouttours.com) or from Fat Tire Bike Tours near the Eiffel Tower (€4/hour, 24 Rue Edgar Faure, fattire-biketoursparis.com, call 01 56 58 10 54 to check availability). Both outfits also offer good bike tours.

Sunday cycling is especially peaceful: The city opens up many districts just for bikes (see paris.fr and search *"Paris respire"* for details).

COMMUNICATING

Telephones

Making Calls: To call France from the US or Canada: Dial 011 (our international access code) + 33 (France's country code) + the local number, without the initial zero. To call France from a European country: Dial 00 (Europe's international access code) + 33 followed by the local number, without the initial zero. To call within France: Just dial the local number (including the initial zero). To call from France to another country: Dial 00, the country code (for example, 1 for the US or Canada), then the area code and number. If you're calling European countries whose phone numbers begin with 0, you'll usually have to omit that 0 when you dial. If you're calling from Europe using your US mobile phone, you may need to dial as if you're calling from the US.

Phoning Inexpensively: Since coin-op pay phones are virtually obsolete, you'll need an international phone card (*carte international,* about €8). With this, you can make reasonably priced local and international calls from any pay phone, a European mobile phone, and even from your hotel phone (though some hotels block these cards or charge a fee). Buy cards at newsstands and *tabac* shops. Tell the vendor where you'll be making the most calls (*"pour les Etats-Unis"*—to America), and he'll select a good-value brand. Calling from your hotel room without a phone card can be a rip-off—ask your hotelier about their rates before you dial.

Mobile Phones and Smartphones: Many US mobile phones work in Europe. Expect to pay around $1.50 a minute for phone calls and 30 cents per text message (somewhat less if you sign up for an international

Useful Phone Numbers

Police: Tel. 17
Emergency Medical Assistance: Tel. 15
Directory Assistance (some English spoken): Tel. 12
US Consulate and Embassy: Tel. 01 43 12 22 22, emergency services
    Mon-Fri 9:00-11:00, 4 Avenue Gabriel, Mo: Concorde, france.us
    embassy.gov
Canadian Consulate and Embassy: Tel. 01 44 43 29 02, 35 Avenue
    Montaigne, Mo: Franklin D. Roosevelt, amb-canada.fr
Collect Calls to the US: Tel. 00 00 11

calling plan with your service provider). It's easy to buy a phone in Europe, which costs more up front but is cheaper by the call. You'll find mobile-phone stores selling cheap phones (for as little as $20 plus minutes) and SIM cards, at Charles de Gaulle airport, major train stations, and throughout Paris.

Smartphones give you access to the Internet and travel-oriented apps—helpful for planning your sightseeing, emailing hotels, and staying in touch. You can make free or cheap phone calls using Skype (sign up at skype.com), Google Talk (google.com/talk), or Facetime (preloaded on many Apple devices). City Maps 2Go ($2, available from iTunes) gives you good searchable maps even when you're not online.

To avoid sky-high fees for data roaming, disable data roaming entirely, and only go online when you have free Wi-Fi (e.g., at your hotel or in a café). Or you could sign up for an international data plan for the duration of your trip: $30 typically buys about 100 megabytes—enough to view 100 websites or send/receive 1,000 emails.

For more information, talk to your service provider or see ricksteves. com/phoning.

Internet Access and Wi-Fi

Most hotels offer some form of free or cheap Internet access—either a shared computer in the lobby or Wi-Fi in the room. Otherwise, your hotelier can point you to the nearest Internet café. You'll also find plenty of Wi-Fi hotspots at cafés and a few museums. In a Parisian café, Wi-Fi works just like at home—you order something, then ask the waiter for the Wi-Fi ("wee-fee") password (mot de passe; moh duh pahs). Most public parks offer free Wi-Fi (look for purple Zone Wi-Fi signs) with an easy one-time registration (start by selecting the Wi-Fi network, usually called "Paris_WIFI"). The Orange network also has many hotspots; you can buy a plan or sign up for a free two-hour pass (orange-wifi.com).

Snail Mail

You can arrange for mail delivery to your hotel (allow 10 days for a letter to arrive). Federal Express makes pricey two-day deliveries. Sending a package home via the French Post Office's Colissimo XL mailing box costs about €40 for 12 pounds.

SIGHTSEEING TIPS

Hours: Hours of sights can change unexpectedly; confirm the latest times from a TI, or at the sight's website, or the general website parisinfo.com. Many sights stop admitting people 30-60 minutes before closing time, and guards start shooing people out before the actual closing time, so don't save the best for last.

What to Expect: Important sights such as the Louvre have metal detectors or conduct bag searches that will slow your entry. Others require you to check (for free) daypacks and coats. To avoid checking a small backpack, carry it under your arm like a purse as you enter.

Photos and videos are normally allowed, but flashes or tripods usually are not. Many sights offer guided tours and rent audioguides (€4-7). Expect changes—artwork can be in restoration or on tour. Most have an on-site café.

Discounts: Many sights offer free or reduced admission for children under 18 and for students (with International Student Identity Cards, isic.org). Senior discounts are generally only for EU residents, but it's worth asking—"Réduction troisième âge?" Some sights are free (and crowded) on the first Sunday of the month (Louvre, Orsay, Rodin, Cluny, Pompidou Center), while others offer discounts if you enter later in the day (Orsay, Orangerie, Army Museum).

Free Rick Steves Audio Tours: I've produced free audio tours of many of Paris' best sights. With a mobile device, you can take me along for the Paris Historic Walk, or your tour of the Louvre, the Orsay, and Versailles. Download them via the Rick Steves Audio Europe smartphone app, ricksteves.com/audioeurope, iTunes, or Google Play.

Paris Museum Pass

For many visitors, the Paris Museum Pass is a time- and money-saver. The pass admits you to many of Paris' most popular sights, and lets you skip the (often long) ticket-buying lines. An added benefit is that you can pop into sights you might not otherwise spend the money for.

A pass covering two consecutive days costs €39; four days is €54; and six days is €69. Buy the pass at participating museums, monuments, FNAC department stores, and TIs. Avoid buying the pass at a major museum (such as the Louvre) with long lines.

Most of Paris' major sights are covered by the pass, including the Louvre, Orsay, Sainte-Chapelle, Picasso Museum, and Versailles. Key sights that are NOT covered are the Eiffel Tower, Montparnasse Tower, Marmottan Museum, Opéra Garnier, and Jacquemart-André Museum. Add up your sightseeing to see if the pass is worth it. The pass can pay for itself with as few as four key admissions in two days. For more info and a full list of covered sights, visit parismuseumpass.com or call 01 44 61 96 60.

To use your pass at sights, boldly walk to the front of the ticket line (after passing security if necessary), hold up your pass, and ask the ticket-taker: *"Entrez, pass?"* (ahn-tray pahs). You'll be ushered directly in.

To make the most of your pass, validate it only when you're ready to tackle the covered sights on consecutive days. Make sure those sights will be open. Sightsee like mad during your "pass" days by visiting sights open late.

Avoiding Lines with Advance Tickets: Even without a Museum Pass, you can still skip ticket lines at many places with long lines. You can buy individual *"coupe-file"* (line-cutting) tickets at TIs and FNAC department stores. Several sights, such as the Eiffel Tower and Monet's gardens at Giverny, sell advance tickets online.

THEFT AND EMERGENCIES

Theft: While violent crime is rare in the city center, thieves (mainly pickpockets) thrive near famous monuments and on the Métro. Be alert to the possibility of theft, even when you're absorbed in the wonder and newness of Paris. Be on guard when crowds press together, especially at tourist sights, while you're preoccupied at ticket windows, and while boarding and leaving buses and subways. Assume any beggar or friendly petitioner is really a pickpocket, and that any commotion in a crowd is a distraction to pickpockets. Watch out for a common scam where a stranger "finds" a ring and offers to sell it to you. Smartphones are thief magnets. I keep my valuables—passport, credit cards, crucial documents, and large amounts of cash—in a money belt that I tuck under my beltline. Muggings are rare, but if you're out late, avoid dimly lit, empty places, such as the dark riverfront embankments.

Dial 17 for English-speaking police help. Claim lost property at the police station (36 Rue des Morillons, Mo: Convention, tel. 01 45 31 14 80). To replace a passport, file a police report, then call your embassy to make an appointment.

Medical Help: In France, dial 15 for an ambulance. For minor ailments, first visit a pharmacy (marked by a green cross), where qualified technicians routinely diagnose and prescribe. For more serious problems, ask your hotelier for assistance. Many doctors speak English. The American Hospital is at 63 Boulevard Victor Hugo in the Neuilly suburb (Mo: Porte Maillot, tel. 01 46 41 25 25). SOS Doctors make house calls to hotels or homes for about €50-70 (tel. 01 47 07 77 77). A good list of English-speaking doctors is available on the website of the US Embassy in Paris (france.usembassy.gov).

ACTIVITIES

Shopping

Chic Paris has a tradition of marketing some of the world's most elegant, trendy, and overpriced clothes, jewels, and foods. The shops with their window displays are works of art themselves. Stroll some of the fashionable neighborhoods and indulge in a little window-shopping, which the French call *faire du lèche-vitrines*—"window-licking."

Most shops are open Monday to Saturday 10:00-19:00.

Shopping Etiquette: Entering a small shop, greet the clerk with *"Bonjour, Madame (or Mademoiselle or Monsieur),"* and bid them *"Au revoir"* when leaving. Ask before handling clothing—*"Je peux?"* means "Can I?" It's OK if you're "just looking"—*"Je regarde, merci."*

Grand Department Stores: Paris invented the modern department store—different items under a single roof, with fixed prices—and several venerable places are still in business. The Galeries Lafayette flagship store, near the Opéra Garnier, features a sensational belle époque dome, a rooftop viewpoint, and fashion shows every Friday at 15:00 from March through October (40 Boulevard Haussman, galerieslafayette.com, reserve fashion show at tel. 01 42 82 30 25). A block west is Printemps, with cheaper prices and a better rooftop view.

Place de la Madeleine Neighborhood (Mo: Madeleine; ✪ see map on page 161): This ritzy area forms a miracle mile of gourmet food shops, four-star hotels, glittering jewelry stores, exclusive clothing boutiques, and people who spend more on clothes in a day than I do all year. Stroll counterclockwise around Place de la Madeleine, with its Greek-temple-esque church. Start with the bastion of gourmet food stores, Fauchon. Peruse the deli and bakery, then cross the street to Fauchon's other outlet, and stroll downstairs to the wine cellar to consider a €3,500 bottle of Cognac.

Continuing around the square, don't miss Fauchon's rival, Hédiard (founded 1854), whose small red containers are popular souvenirs. At La Maison des Truffe, smell those truffles and ponder how something so ugly can cost €2,500 a pound. Continue past a tea store and a caviar store—fish eggs can sell for up to €8,000 a pound.

To extend this walk, stroll down Rue Royale and turn left on Rue St. Honoré, then left again on Rue de Castiglione. End the walk on the *très* elegant square, Place Vendôme, home to upper-crust jewelry stores and the Hôtel Ritz.

Sèvres-Babylone to St. Sulpice (Mo: Sèvres-Babylone; ✪ see map on page 156): For Left Bank swank, start at the Bon Marché department store, Paris' oldest. Walk down Rue de Sèvres, and consider a drink at the terribly cool Au Savignon Café (#10). Continue on to the half-man-half-horse statue (ouch)—you're at a pinwheel intersection of several boutique-lined streets worth exploring. When you're ready, turn right on Rue du Vieux Colombier and head to St. Sulpice Church. To finish the walk, continue past the church on Rue St. Sulpice and turn left on Rue de Seine, to find Gérard Mulot's *pâtisserie* (#76) with arguably Paris' best pastries.

Flea Markets: The granddaddy of oversized garage sales is the Puces St. Ouen, on Paris' northern fringe. Vendors in covered alleys sell everything from flamingos to faucets, but mostly antiques. It runs Saturday 9:00-18:00, Sunday 10:00-18:00, and Monday 11:00-17:00. From the Porte de Clignancourt Métro station, walk straight out of the station and pass under the freeway overpass. Veer left on Rue des Rosiers—the main "spine" of the sprawling market—and explore from there. Some find the market a delightful melting pot; for others it's a gritty, crowded, overwhelming experience, with thieves on the prowl. For a smaller, less-touristed flea market, try the Puces de Vanves (Sat-Sun only, 7:00-17:00, Mo: Porte de Vanves).

Open-Air Produce Markets: These are museums for people-watchers. Many neighborhoods have one street or square for traffic-free shopping, overflowing with flowers, produce, fish vendors, and cafés. Most are open all day Tuesday through Saturday (except at lunch 13:00-15:00), and Sunday morning.

Rue Cler is refined and upscale (Mo: Ecole Militaire, ✪ see the Rue Cler Walk, page 111). Rue Montorgueil, a half-mile northeast of the Louvre, has a more local scene and the elegant covered arcade, passage du grand Cerf, nearby (Mo: Etienne Marcel). Rue Mouffetard, hiding several blocks behind the Panthéon, starts on picturesque Place Contrescarpe and gets grittier the farther downhill you go (Mo: Censier Daubenton). In the heart of the Left Bank, try Rue de Seine and Rue de Buci (Mo: Odéon).

Souvenirs: You won't need a guidebook to find plenty of shops selling "I Heart Paris" T-shirts, *Mona Lisa* mouse pads, and Eiffel Tower keychains—especially along Rue de Rivoli (near the Louvre) and Rue d'Arcole (north of Notre-Dame). The riverfront stalls near Notre-Dame are classy and picturesque if higher-priced.

Getting a VAT Refund: If you purchase more than €175 worth of goods at a single store, you may be eligible to get a refund of the 20 percent Value-Added Tax (VAT). Have the store fill out the paperwork, then, at the airport, get it stamped by Customs and processed by a VAT refund company. At Charles de Gaulle, you'll find them at the check-in area, or ask for help at an orange ADP info desk. Get more details from your merchant or see ricksteves.com/vat.

Customs for American Shoppers: You are allowed to take home $800 worth of items per person duty-free, once every 30 days. You can also bring in duty-free a liter of alcohol.

As for food, you can take home many processed and packaged foods (e.g., vacuum-packed cheeses, chocolate, mustard) but no fresh produce or meats (canned pâtés are an exception). Any liquid-containing foods must be packed in checked luggage, a potential recipe for disaster. To check customs rules and duty rates, visit help.cbp.gov.

Nightlife

Paris is brilliant after dark. Perhaps the best after-dark activity is to enjoy a leisurely meal, then stroll historic streets, past floodlit squares and fountains.

The *Pariscope* magazine (€0.40 at any newsstand) offers a complete weekly listing of events. It's in French, but it's easy to decipher what's going on in the worlds of *Musique, Cinéma, Théâtre, Arts, etc.*

Jazz and Blues Clubs: Paris has been a jazz capital since the Roaring 20s. At most clubs, expect to pay (about) a €20 entry plus €7 per drink. Caveau de la Huchette, in the Latin Quarter near Notre-Dame, is a steamy cellar for hot jazz and frenzied swing dancing (5 Rue de la Huchette, tel. 01 43 26 65 05, caveaudelahuchette.fr). Rue des Lombards, a street in central Paris (Mo: Châtelet), is a teeming two-block-long hive of nightlife. The plush Au Duc des Lombards club offers high-class jazz in a theater-like setting (42 Rue des Lombards, tel. 01 42 33 22 88, ducdeslombards.fr). Le Sunside, just a block away, has two different stages (60 Rue des Lombards, tel. 01 40 26 46 60, sunset-sunside.com).

Classical Concerts: Several historic churches regularly host concerts (mostly Baroque-style chamber music) from March to November: Sainte-Chapelle, St. Sulpice, St. Germain-des-Prés, La Madeleine, St. Eustache, and St. Julien-le-Pauvre. Sainte-Chapelle is especially worthwhile for the pleasure of hearing Mozart, Bach, or Vivaldi, surrounded by the stained glass of the tiny church (it's unheated—bring a sweater). Buy tickets there or make reservations (tel. 01 42 77 65 65 or 06 67 30 65 65, euromusicproductions.fr).

The Salle Pleyel (north of the Arc de Triomphe) hosts world-class international concerts at high prices (252 Rue du Faubourg St.-Honoré, Mo: Ternes, tel 01 42 56 13 13, sallepleyel.fr).

Opera is performed at the massive modern opera house, the Opéra Bastille (Mo: Bastille). The Opéra Garnier, Paris' first opera house, hosts opera and ballet in a grand belle époque setting (Mo: Opéra). Get tickets for either opera house at tel. 08 92 89 90 90, operadeparis.fr, or at their box offices.

Movies: Many theaters run movies in their original language (look for *"v.o."—version originale*). Cinemas cluster around Mo: Odéon. Enjoy the big movie palaces on the Champs-Elysées.

Rowdy Bars and Clubs: For late-night partying (after 21:00), try the Rue de Lappe—take the Metro to Bastille, head north and follow the noise. Other areas are around Rue Vieille du Temple in the Marais (Mo: St. Paul), rue des Lombards (Mo: Châtelet), and Rue des Canettes and Guisarde (Mo: St. Sulpice).

Museums: To check which museums have later opening hours on some nights, ✪ see the Paris at a Glance sidebar on page 10. For a list of free wine-and-cheese art gallery openings (called *vernissages*), check paris.artalog.net.

Tours by Night: Consider a Seine River cruise or bus tour. Two companies that take up to three people on informal, fun, off-beat tours in old Deux Chevaux cars are Paris Authentic (mobile 06 64 50 44 19, parisauthentic.com) and 4 Roues Sous 1 Parapluie (mobile 06 67 32 26 68, 4roues-sous 1parapluie.com). Do-it-yourselfers could snag a taxi and make their own scenic tour—from Notre-Dame to the Eiffel Tower along the Left Bank, then returning along the Right Bank (figure about €50 for a one-hour loop, split by up to four passengers).

Night Scenes: The Eiffel Tower viewed from Place du Trocadéro is spectacular, and the Trocadéro itself is a festival of hawkers, gawkers, roller-bladers, and entertainers. The Champs-Elysées and Arc de Triomphe glitter after dark. Ile St. Louis (Mo: Pont Marie) is quiet and romantic; perfect for dinner, for sampling Paris' best ice cream shops, and for a stroll to floodlit Notre-Dame.

Get your Left Bank buzz in the area around Place St. Germain-des-Prés and Odéon (Mo: St. Germain-des-Prés and Odéon), full of famous cafés, cinemas, and night owls prowling along Rue des Canettes, Rue Guisarde, and Rue de Buci. Montmartre is touristy but lively, and a bit dicey

Practicalities

Those Parisians

The idea that Parisians are "mean and cold and refuse to speak English" is an out-of-date preconception left over from the days of Charles de Gaulle. Parisians are as friendly as any other people, and no more disagreeable than New Yorkers.

Parisians may appear cold when they're actually being polite and formal, respecting the fine points of culture and tradition. (From their view, those ever-smiling Americans, while friendly, are somewhat insincere.) And let's face it: It's tough to keep on smiling when you've been crushed by a Big Mac, Mickey-Moused by Disney, and drowned in instant coffee.

Like many big cities, Paris is a massive melting pot of people from all over France plus recent immigrants. Your evening hotel receptionist may speak French with an accent.

To appreciate the French—slow down. Observe the French pace of life. Despite its size and modernity, Paris maintains a genuine village feel. People still hold the door open for you in the Métro. People share family news with their neighborhood grocer. And on warm summer nights, the streets and cafés are full of happy Parisians in love with life.

at night. For old-time cabaret ambience, consider Au Lapin Agile (€24, shows in French only, tel. 01 46 06 85 87, au-lapin-agile.com), and end the evening in front of Sacré-Cœur Basilica for the glorious city view.

Connecting with the Culture

Make your trip more personal through one-on-one contact with real live English-speaking Parisians. A group called Meeting the French organizes dinners and workplace tours (meetingthefrench.com). Paris Greeter's volunteers guide you through "their" Paris (parisgreeters.fr). Ô Château offers fun, informal wine-tasting classes (o-chateau.com). Cooking schools have pricey demonstration courses—the most famous is Le Cordon Bleu (lcb-paris.com). Parler Paris lets you practice conversational French in a relaxed environment (parlerparlor.com). Or check out the people-to-people events at meetup.com.

Tours

Seine Cruises: Several companies run one-hour, €13 boat cruises on the Seine, best by night, and worth checking out for their dinner cruises. Bateaux-Mouches has large, open-topped, often-crowded boats departing from the Pont de l'Alma (bateaux-mouches.com). Others are Bateaux Parisiens (from the Eiffel Tower, bateauxparisiens.com) and Vedettes du Pont Neuf (from Pont Neuf, vedettesdupontneuf.com). Batobus allows you to get on and off, making their day passes worthwhile for point-A-to-B travel (batobus.com).

Bus Tours: Hop-on, hop-off bus tours let you ride through Paris on an open-air bus. Hop on at any of the stops along their loop routes, pay as you board (€31 for a day), ride awhile, hop off to sightsee, then catch the next one to carry on. Two similar companies are in business—L'Open Tour (paris-opentour.com) and Les Car Rouges (carsrouges.com). City Vision offers uninspired bus tours at night, and basic excursions outside the city, e.g., to D-Day beaches or the Loire (pariscityvision.com).

Guided Tours: For walking tours of Paris' history, art, and neighborhoods, try Paris Walks (paris-walks.com). Context Paris is serious and intellectual (contextparis.com). Fat Tire Bike Tours' Classic Walk is the antithesis—low-brow and high-fun, while their Easy Pass interior tours of major sights let you skip the lines (classicwalksparis.com).

Bike tours guide a dozen cyclists on breezy excursions through neighborhoods. Try Bike About Tours, near Notre-Dame (bikeabouttours.com) or Fat Tire Bike Tours, near the Eiffel Tower (fattirebiketoursparis.com).

If you'd like a private guide (around €200/half day), try Arnaud Servignat (tel. 06 68 80 29 05, french-guide.com), Thierry Gauduchon (tel. 06 19 07 30 77, tgauduchon@gmail.com), or Elizabeth Van Hest (tel. 01 43 41 47 31, elisa.guide@gmail.com).

Ricksteves.com

This Pocket Guide is one of dozens of titles in my series of guidebooks on European travel. I also produce a public television series, *Rick Steves' Europe,* and a public radio show, *Travel with Rick Steves.* My website, ricksteves.com, offers a wealth of free travel information including videos and podcasts of my shows, audio tours of Europe's great sights, travel forums, guidebook updates, my travel blog, and my guide to European rail-passes—plus an online travel store and information on our tours of Europe.

How Was Your Trip? If you'd like to share your tips, concerns, and discoveries after using this book, please fill out the survey at ricksteves.com/feedback. It helps us and fellow travelers.

Practicalities

French Survival Phrases

When using the phonetics, try to nasalize the <u>n</u> sound.

English	French	Phonetics
Good day.	Bonjour.	bohn-zhoor
Mrs. / Mr.	Madame / Monsieur	mah-dahm / muhs-yur
Do you speak English?	Parlez-vous anglais?	par-lay-voo ahn-glay
Yes. / No.	Oui. / Non.	wee / nohn
I understand.	Je comprends.	zhuh kohn-prahn
I don't understand.	Je ne comprends pas.	zhuh nuh kohn-prahn pah
Please.	S'il vous plaît.	see voo play
Thank you.	Merci.	mehr-see
I'm sorry.	Désolé.	day-zoh-lay
Excuse me.	Pardon.	par-dohn
(No) problem.	(Pas de) problème.	(pah duh) proh-blehm
It's good.	C'est bon.	say bohn
Goodbye.	Au revoir.	oh vwahr
one / two	un / deux	uhn / duh
three / four	trois / quatre	twah / kah-truh
five / six	cinq / six	sank / sees
seven / eight	sept / huit	seht / weet
nine / ten	neuf / dix	nuhf / dees
How much is it?	Combien?	kohn-bee-an
Write it?	Ecrivez?	ay-kree-vay
Is it free?	C'est gratuit?	say grah-twee
Included?	Inclus?	an-klew
Where can I buy / find...?	Où puis-je acheter / trouver...?	oo pwee-zhuh ah-shuh-tay / troo-vay
I'd like / We'd like...	Je voudrais / Nous voudrions...	zhuh voo-dray / noo voo-dree-ohn
...a room.	...une chambre.	ewn shahn-bruh
...a ticket to ___.	...un billet pour ___.	uhn bee-yay poor
Is it possible?	C'est possible?	say poh-see-bluh
Where is...?	Où est...?	oo ay
...the train station	...la gare	lah gar
...the bus station	...la gare routière	lah gar root-yehr
...tourist information	...l'office du tourisme	loh-fees dew too-reez-muh
Where are the toilets?	Où sont les toilettes?	oo sohn lay twah-leht
men	hommes	ohm
women	dames	dahm
left / right	à gauche / à droite	ah gohsh / ah dwaht
straight	tout droit	too dwah
When does this open / close?	Ça ouvre / ferme à quelle heure?	sah oo-vruh / fehrm ah kehl ur
At what time?	À quelle heure?	ah kehl ur
Just a moment.	Un moment.	uhn moh-mahn
now / soon / later	maintenant / bientôt / plus tard	man-tuh-nahn / bee-an-toh / plew tar
today / tomorrow	aujourd'hui / demain	oh-zhoor-dwee / duh-man

In the Restaurant

I'd like / We'd like...	Je voudrais / Nous voudrions...	zhuh voo-dray / noo voo-dree-ohn
...to reserve...	...réserver...	ray-zehr-vay
...a table for one / two.	...une table pour un / deux.	ewn tah-bluh poor uhn / duh
Non-smoking.	Non fumeur.	nohn few-mur
Is this seat free?	C'est libre?	say lee-bruh
The menu (in English), please.	La carte (en anglais), s'il vous plaît.	lah kart (ahn ahn-glay) see voo play
service (not) included	service (non) compris	sehr-vees (nohn) kohn-pree
to go	à emporter	ah ahn-por-tay
with / without	avec / sans	ah-vehk / sahn
and / or	et / ou	ay / oo
special of the day	plat du jour	plah dew zhoor
specialty of the house	spécialité de la maison	spay-see-ah-lee-tay duh lah may-zohn
appetizers	hors-d'oeuvre	or-duh-vruh
first course (soup, salad)	entrée	ahn-tray
main course (meat, fish)	plat principal	plah pran-see-pahl
bread	pain	pan
cheese	fromage	froh-mahzh
sandwich	sandwich	sahnd-weech
soup	soupe	soop
salad	salade	sah-lahd
meat	viande	vee-ahnd
chicken	poulet	poo-lay
fish	poisson	pwah-sohn
seafood	fruits de mer	frwee duh mehr
mineral water	eau minérale	oh mee-nay-rahl
tap water	l'eau du robinet	loh dew roh-bee-nay
milk	lait	lay
(orange) juice	jus (d'orange)	zhew (doh-rahnzh)
coffee	café	kah-fay
tea	thé	tay
wine	vin	van
red / white	rouge / blanc	roozh / blahn
glass / bottle	verre / bouteille	vehr / boo-teh-ee
beer	bière	bee-ehr
Cheers!	Santé!	sahn-tay
More. / Another.	Plus. / Un autre.	plew / uhn oh-truh
The same.	La même chose.	lah mehm shohz
The bill, please.	L'addition, s'il vous plaît.	lah-dee-see-ohn see voo play
tip	pourboire	poor-bwar
Delicious!	Délicieux!	day-lee-see-uh

For more user-friendly French phrases, check out *Rick Steves' French Phrase Book and Dictionary* or *Rick Steves' French, Italian & German Phrase Book*.

INDEX

PHOTO CREDITS

Title Page
© Sborisov/Dreamstime.com

Historic Paris Walk
p. 14 © sborisov/123rf.com; p. 17, right © Bryan Busovicki/123rf.com; p. 24, right © Konrad Glogowski/flickr.com; p. 33, right © Luke Daniek/istockphoto.com; p. 38, right © Ionut Dobrescu/123rf.com; p. 42, right, Pont-Neuf-Partiel.jpg, commons.wikimedia.org

Louvre Tour
p. 48, right © James Shin/flickr.com; p. 54, left © The Art Gallery Collection / Alamy; right © INTERFOTO/Alamt; p. 57, left, The Yorck Project*, commons.wikimedia.org; p. 58, The Yorck Project*, commons.wikimedia.org; p. 59 © The Art Gallery Collection / Alamy; p. 61, left, © Dennis Hallinan / Alamy; p. 61, right, The Yorck Project*, commons.wikimedia.org; p. 63 © classicpaintings/Alamy; p. 65, left, The Yorck Project*, commons.wikimedia.org

Orsay Museum Tour
p. 69 © classicpaintings/Alamy; p. 72, right, The Yorck Project*, commons.wikimedia.org; © p. 77, right, © RMN-Grand Palais/Art Resources, NY; p. 80 © Masterpics / Alamy; p. 82, left © Peter Barritt / Alamy; p. 82, right, The Yorck Project*, commons.wikimedia.org; p. 83, The Yorck Project*, commons.wikimedia.org; p. 86, The Yorck Project*, commons.wikimedia.org, p. 91 © Chris Heller/Alamy, p. 92, right © Purestock, p. 93 © Masterpics/Alamy; p. 95 © B&Y Photography/Alamy

Eiffel Tower Tour
p. 100 © Domen Colja/123rf.com; p. 101, right © Jose I. Soto/Dreamstime.com

Versailles Day Trip
p. 121 © Adriano Rubino/123rf.com; p. 126, left © Jose I. Soto/Dreamstimes.com; p. 130, © North Wind Picture Archives / Alamy; p. 138, left © Cosmin - Constantin Sava/Dreamstime.com; p. 145, right © Jose I. Soto/Dreamstimes.com

Sights
p. 146 © Elena Elisseeva/123rf.com; p. 162, right and p. 170, right © Dominic Arizona Bonuccelli

Sleeping
p. 173 © Elena Elisseeva/123rf.com

Eating
p. 182 © Outline205 | Dreamstime.com

Photo Credits, continued on next page

Practicalities
p. 196 © Ritu Jethani/123rf.com

Additional photography by Rick Steves, Ben Cameron, Mary Ann Cameron, Rich Earl, Cameron Hewitt, Dave C. Hoerlein, Pat O'Connor, Gene Openshaw, Carol Ries, Gretchen Strauch, Bruce VanDeventer, Laura VanDeventer, Rob Unck.

Unless otherwise noted, copyrights apply to photographs of artwork.

Audio Europe

Rick's Free Travel App

Get your FREE **Rick Steves Audio Europe**™ app to enjoy…

- Dozens of self-guided tours of Europe's top museums, sights and historic walks
- Hundreds of tracks filled with cultural insights and sightseeing tips from Rick's radio interviews
- All organized into handy geographic playlists
- For iPhone, iPad, iPod Touch, Android

With Rick whispering in your ear, Europe gets even better.

Join a Rick Steves tour

Enjoy Europe's warmest welcome... with the flexibility and friendship of a small group getting to know Rick's favorite places and people. It all starts with our free tour catalog and DVD.

Great guides, small groups, no grumps.

See more than three dozen itineraries throughout Europe
tours.ricksteves.com

Start your trip at

Free information and great gear to

▶ Plan Your Trip

Browse thousands of articles and a wealth of money-saving tips for planning your dream trip. You'll find up-to-date information on Europe's best destinations, packing smart, getting around, finding rooms, staying healthy, avoiding scams and more.

▶ Eurail Passes

Find out, step-by-step, if a railpass makes sense for your trip—and how to avoid buying more than you need. Get a bunch of free extras!

▶ Graffiti Wall & Travelers Helpline

Learn, ask, share—our online community of savvy travelers is a great resource for first-time travelers to Europe, as well as seasoned pros.

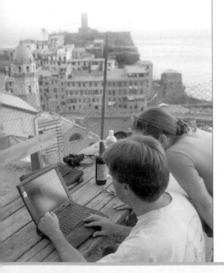

Rick Steves' Europe Through the Back Door, Inc.

Rick Steves

www.ricksteves.com

EUROPE GUIDES

Best of Europe
Eastern Europe
Europe Through the Back Door
Mediterranean Cruise Ports
Northern European Cruise Ports

COUNTRY GUIDES

Croatia & Slovenia
England
France
Germany
Great Britain
Ireland
Italy
Portugal
Scandinavia
Spain
Switzerland

CITY & REGIONAL GUIDES

Amsterdam, Bruges & Brussels
Barcelona
Budapest
Florence & Tuscany
Greece: Athens & the Peloponnese
Istanbul
London
Paris
Prague & the Czech Republic
Provence & the French Riviera

Rome
Venice
Vienna, Salzburg & Tirol

SNAPSHOT GUIDES

Berlin
Bruges & Brussels
Copenhagen & the Best of Denmark
Dublin
Dubrovnik
Hill Towns of Central Italy
Italy's Cinque Terre
Krakow, Warsaw & Gdansk
Lisbon
Madrid & Toledo
Munich, Bavaria & Salzburg
Naples & the Amalfi Coast
Northern Ireland
Norway
Scotland
Sevilla, Granada & Southern Spain
Stockholm

POCKET GUIDES

Amsterdam
Athens
Barcelona
Florence
London
Paris
Rome
Venice

Avalon Travel
a member of the Perseus Books Group
1700 Fourth Street
Berkeley, CA 94710

Printed in China by RR Donnelley
First printing May 2014.

ISBN 978-1-61238-554-9
ISSN 2158-8503

For the latest on Rick's lectures, guidebooks, tours, public radio show, and public television series, contact Europe Through the Back Door, Box 2009, Edmonds, WA 98020, tel. 425/771-8303, fax 425/771-0833, ricksteves.com, or rick@ricksteves.com.

Rick Steves' Europe Through the Back Door
Managing Editor: Risa Laib
Editorial & Production Manager: Jennifer Madison Davis
Editors: Glenn Eriksen, Tom Griffin, Cameron Hewitt, Suzanne Kotz, Cathy Lu, Carrie Shepherd
Researcher: Mary Bouron
Maps & Graphics: Barb Geisler, Sandra Hundacker, David C. Hoerlein, Lauren Mills, Mary Rustad

Avalon Travel
Senior Editor and Series Manager: Madhu Prasher
Editor: Jamie Andrade
Associate Editor: Annette Kohl
Assistant Editor: Maggie Ryan
Copy Editor: Judith Brown
Proofreader: Kelly Lydick
Indexer: Stephen Callahan
Production & Typesetting: McGuire Barber Design
Cover Design: Kimberly Glyder Design
Interior Design: Darren Alessi
Maps & Graphics: Kat Bennett, Mike Morgenfeld, Brice Ticen
Photography: Rick Steves, Steve Smith, David C. Hoerlein, Gene Openshaw, Laura VanDeventer, Cameron Hewitt, Julie Coen, Barb Geisler, Ben Cameron, Ragen Van Sewell, Robyn Cronin, Rob Unck, Carol Ries, Rich Earl, Rachel Worthman (additional photo credits, page 227)
Front Cover Image: Eiffel Tower © Arnaud Chicurel/Getty; Le Metro cafe, Place Maubert, Boulevard St Germain © Izzet Keribar/Getty

ABOUT THE AUTHORS

Rick Steves

Since 1973, Rick Steves has spent 100 days every year exploring Europe. Along with writing and researching a bestselling series of guidebooks, Rick produces a public television series *(Rick Steves' Europe)*, a public radio show *(Travel with Rick Steves)*, and an app and podcast *(Rick Steves Audio Europe)*; writes a nationally syndicated newspaper column; organizes guided tours that take over ten thousand travelers to Europe annually; and offers an information-packed website (www.ricksteves.com). With the help of his hard-working staff of 80 at Europe Through the Back Door—in Edmonds, Washington, just north of Seattle—Rick's mission is to make European travel fun, affordable, and culturally enlightening for Americans.

Connect with Rick: **f** facebook.com/RickSteves 🐦 twitter: @RickSteves

Steve Smith

Steve Smith manages tour planning for Rick Steves' Europe Through the Back Door and has been researching guidebooks with Rick for two decades. Fluent in French, he's lived in France on several occasions, starting when he was seven, and has traveled there annually since 1986. Steve's wife, Karen Lewis Smith, who's an expert on French cuisine and wine, provides invaluable contributions to his books, as do his two children.

Gene Openshaw

Gene Openshaw is a writer, composer, tour guide, and lecturer on art and history. Specializing in writing walking tours of Europe's cultural sights, Gene has co-authored a dozen of Rick's books and contributes to Rick's public television series. As a composer, Gene has written a full-length opera *(Matter)*, a violin sonata, and dozens of songs. He lives near Seattle with his daughter, and roots for the Mariners in good times and bad.

FOLDOUT COLOR MAP

The foldout map on the opposite page includes:
• A map of Paris on one side
• Maps of Greater Paris, France, and Paris Metro on the other side